How To Get An Animation Internship

A Guide that Helps You Apply, Interview, and Get Your Foot Into Show Business

by Eric Bravo

Little Kingdom
Publishing

Bravo Bros. Studio

Copyright

Contents

Dedication

To Mom, Nana, & Brother

For without the love and support from each one of you, I would not have been able to follow my dreams and share my experience with the world.

To Auntie

You are always there to help guide and push me whenever I feel lost. Without you, I wouldn't have the necessary skills or tools to pursue my dreams.

To all of my family & friends

Thank you for believing in me and cheering me on as I pursue this crazy dream of mine.

To Walt Disney & Steve Jobs

Thank you for pushing our culture forward with your innovation and limitless dreaming.

Introduction

Animation has a special place in all of our hearts. It's what most of us grew up watching as children—and continue to watch today. At the age of nine, I often used to visit Pixar's website. I was obsessed with their movies and wanted to know what skills I needed to work there in the future. I knew they dealt with computer graphics, so back then I had my mind set, I'll study computer science! In high school, I enrolled in AP Computer Science, thinking this would lead me to a career at Pixar. Not long into the course, I found out I wasn't interested in Computer Science at all, and my teacher didn't mention animation once! I dreaded going to class and eventually failed it. After this devastating experience, I quietly put my dreams of working in the animation industry away.

Fast-forward to college—I met someone who had interned at DreamWorks twice and Nickelodeon, and was currently interviewing to intern at Pixar. Needless to say, I was curious. I had so many questions. *How did he work for all of these animation studios as a junior? How did he get an internship in Southern California when we were 7 hours away in Northern California? Did he take time off school? Does the school even allow it?*

I went home and looked on Pixar's website. I'd forgotten that as a college student, I could apply to their programs. My excitement came and went, as I quickly became confused about what these internship roles were. I had yet more questions. *Did I have the necessary skills and experience to be a production intern? What does a production intern even do?*

As children and young adults, we enjoy this beautiful art form, but most never consider a career in it. I for one assumed that you had to be a talented drawer or a computer wiz kid to be in the industry, which I later found out wasn't true. But when you're starting out, the question is: how does one get into what seems like an exclusive industry? Can non-artists be part of the industry? What kind of jobs are there?

All of these questions can be answered through an internship. During an internship, you'll gain knowledge, but more importantly—**experience**. Internships get you started with networking and exploring different departments, and can even be a stepping stone for a job in the industry. But then comes another road block. So the real question is: *How do you get an animation internship?*

Animation jobs are some of the most competitive to attain and internships are the best way to improve your chances of getting one. With this book, you'll be able to set your application apart and know how to tailor your resume to increase the likelihood of gaining an internship. Animation has become a huge industry. It's an exciting world that most of us love to be in and an internship is the best way in!

About This Book

This book was inspired by a blog that I started called The StoryBoard Room. I created the blog to offer knowledge and advice to college students who want to get into the animation industry, but have no idea where to start. I know first-hand just how hard it is to find any information on getting an internship in the animation industry, so I wanted to provide a place where students or anyone interested could visit and get their questions answered from industry professionals. It worked, and the blog was so popular that I am now inundated with questions. So, I decided to write this book to answer the sheer number of questions and to give my personal advice, as it isn't possible to reply to each and every e-mail. As much as I'd like to build a personal connection with every student, this book is a far better solution as I can go into detail and provide you with as much information as possible. This book contains all of my knowledge and experience laid out for you to use as a blueprint when trying to get into the animation industry. I'll also give you a "behind the scenes" look from people who work in the industry—with interviews from employees and students who have interned at major animation studios such as Nickelodeon Animation Studio, DreamWorks Animation Studio, Walt Disney Animation Studio, Cartoon Network, LAIKA, and Industrial Light & Magic. These interviews cover various departments in the animation industry and how they went from an intern to an industry professional.

All in all, I hope this book relieves the stress that comes with pursing an internship in the animation industry. Just know, I can't promise you an internship. That's ultimately up to you and how badly you want it. What I can give you is helpful tips and insightful knowledge from industry professionals, which took me years to accumulate, to help you on your path into show business.

I've built many relationships with recruiters and I have gathered solid knowledge of what entertainment studios look for in an intern. Take what you need from this book and disregard what you don't. Remember, everyone has their own path. My goal is to show you what I have done so you can study and learn from it, and hopefully succeed even more than I have. Stay focused and don't give up! Your time will come.

If you'd like to stay updated, be sure to follow my blog *The Storyboard Room*, which you can find at www.eric-bravo.com/the-storyboard-room.

Who This Book Is For

I'm assuming that most of you reading this are college students. I understand that you have other things on your plate, like going to class, studying, and having a social life. So I'm going to make this book simple, straight to the point, and easy to digest. I'll try my best to give you digestible insight without too much fluff!

I'd also like to say that this book focuses and is geared towards students at an accredited degree-granting college or university. The reason being, most animation internships require you to be a student attending a degree-granting college or university. Sorry to break it to you high schoolers, the major studios do not accept any high school students for internships (but if you're reading this book already, kudos to you! You'll be more than prepared when it's your time to apply). The major studios only accept junior and senior students as of now. Depending on how many credits you have already taken, you can be considered a junior even if you are in your first or second year.

For international students, proper work authorization is needed to be employed within the United States, so you must be able to provide such documents.

Most studios accept students who are enrolled in graduate or law school. However, I won't be speaking about graduate or law student internships, as I haven't personally attained an internship this way; however, the principle information here can still be applied.

Also, programs are constantly growing and are being upgraded as requirements change. So be sure to read the studio's requirements section to make sure you qualify. For example, studios are now letting recent graduates apply for internships, something that wasn't allowed after my graduation.

How To Read This Book

I designed this book to be used as a guide, making it easy for you to quickly reference a topic or section. I do recommend reading the book all the way through first, so you can get a general idea of the internship process and familiarize yourself with it. Afterward, you can skip to any section that you may need help with or want to improve in.

The Q & A sections are there to inspire and give you insight from people who were in your position and who have successful attained an internship and a position in the animation industry, but you may skip them if you choose.

My Story

How did I intern at Warner Bros. Records, Nickelodeon Animation Studio, and DreamWorks Animation Studio all in one year? First, I would like to clear the air. No, I am not the son of an executive. No, I did not have an "in" or know anyone in the industry and no, I was not a 4.0 student or remotely close to being top of my class. Heck, I wasn't even an animation or film major.

What I did have was two things. The first was a strong passion and love for entertainment, because you can't be great at something you hate. The second was being persistent. I was rejected many times and for many years. It wasn't until my <u>fifth</u> year in college when things started working out for me. The passion and love kept me sane when I felt I was hitting a brick wall, and the persistence kept me pushing until I finally broke through. Without these two qualities, you won't get far. The interview below will give you a better sense of my story, who I am, and how I was able to intern at three major studios in one year.

Q & A With Eric Bravo

- Creator & Writer of Nickelodeon's *The Outsiders*

- Founder of Bravo Bros. Studio

- Financial Analyst at Lionsgate Entertainment

- Mapping Operations Associate on Google's Self-Driving Car Project

- Production Intern on *Penguins of Madagascar* at DreamWorks Animation

- Vault Intern at Nickelodeon Animation Studio

- International Marketing Intern at Warner Bros. Records

Prior to my animation career, I initially wanted to pursue a career in the music industry. I prolonged my graduation date to intern in the International Marketing department at Warner Bros. Records (WBR). After the WBR internship, I was curious to see whether I could intern at a childhood dream studio, so I decided to apply to Nickelodeon's internship program the following semester. I was accepted to Nickelodeon (ranked as one of Forbes's top 10 internships) and there I found my passion for animation. I went from a Vault intern to eventually being a creator and writer of my very own cartoon short, *The Outsiders*. I also got an opportunity to work on the movie *Penguins of Madagascar* at DreamWorks Animation Studio.

During this internship stint, I attended UC Davis, where I got a Bachelor of Science degree in Managerial Economics. After college, I got an incredible opportunity to make a cartoon short as part of Nickelodeon's Animated Shorts Program while working simultaneously at Google on their Self-Driving Car Project. I am now an author, travel blogger, landscape and cityscape photographer, and a financial analyst at Lionsgate, and the founder of Bravo Bros. Studio. In the following interview, you can find out more about me and what I do, based on common questions I've been asked over the years.

Q: WHAT COLLEGE DID I ATTEND AND WHAT WAS MY MAJOR? DID THIS HELP WITH MY PURSUIT IN THE ENTERTAINMENT INDUSTRY?

I attended UC Santa Cruz for two years, then transferred to UC Davis for the last three years of college (yes, I was a super senior!). I majored in Managerial Economics, which is essentially a business degree.

I honestly feel that my major didn't help get me into the entertainment industry. However, it has been a great conversation starter for interviews, since there are very few economics students trying to get into animation.

Even though my major didn't help much, school was a great asset in my pursuit of working in the entertainment industry, because you must be a student to get an animation internship. I was also involved in a business fraternity (Delta Sigma Pi), which taught me valuable interview skills.

Q: WHEN DID I KNOW I WANTED TO BE IN THE ENTERTAINMENT/ANIMATION INDUSTRY AND WHAT EVENTS LED ME TO CHOOSE IT?

As a kid, I always knew I wanted to do something in entertainment or film-related, but I never knew what exactly. I had many creative hobbies, but I never really acted on them until my study aboard trip to Madrid, which was during my fifth year of college. On that trip, I meet two super creative classmates. They were both photographers, musicians, and writers. Just being around them and seeing their work gave me the confidence and inspiration to pursue my creative interest. This spark eventually led me into entertainment and animation.

One of these super-talented, creative classmates was Uyen Cao. She's a designer at Forbes and Time, a photographer, and musician. You can find her at www.uyenthoaicao.com.

Q: DID ANYONE/ANYTHING INSPIRE ME TO FOLLOW MY PASSION FOR ENTERTAINMENT/ANIMATION?

Walt Disney, undoubtedly. My mom is a huge Mickey Mouse fan, so we grew up with Disney everything—I was always surrounded by it! I loved doing research on Walt Disney for school projects, because it intrigued me how this man had built a multi-media empire with just a cartoon character. I hope to inspire and help kids one day just as he did.

Q: HOW DID I LAND THE INTERNSHIP AT WARNER BROS. RECORDS?

I landed the WBR internship by applying as an off-season intern. An off-season intern means during the Fall or Spring semester, not Summer, like most internships are. I really wanted to get into the music industry and had applied for every internship at the record labels for years. However, I'd never hear anything back, which made sense really, considering I had no experience in the music industry. It wasn't until I was studying at UC Davis that something clicked inside me. I realized all I had to do was go to my school's radio station and volunteer there. I didn't need any experience to do that, and since it was volunteer work, they needed all the help they could get. It was a win-win.

After updating my resume with this work experience, I got three interviews for three different positions at WBR. They were for Video Production, Marketing, and International Marketing positions. The Video Production internship required a short film demonstrating my editing skills, so I grabbed my friend and went out to shoot one. The other two positions just required an interview.

I got a call back for two interviews, but I encountered a slight problem there. WBR is in Burbank, CA, and I was back home in Northern California at the time. I know I could have asked for a Skype interview instead, but I interview better in person. So, although it sounds crazy just for an internship interview, but I ended up booking a roundtrip same day ticket to LAX, and off I went to Burbank in my suit and all. I took an airport shuttle from LAX to WBR. I did both of my interviews back to back and flew home that same night. It was kind of surreal, but I really wanted the internship, so it was worth it. The next day, the International Marketing team offered me the internship and I gladly accepted.

Q: WHAT DID I DO AS AN INTERNATIONAL MARKETING INTERN?

Honestly, a ton! The music industry is a very fast-paced environment. It was the toughest internship that I've ever had, but it was also the internship I learned the most from. I really developed and honed a solid office skill set, such as handling phone calls and multitasking, which I use in every job.

My daily tasks included handling a lot of highly sensitive information. I was in charge of gathering sales data for all of Warner's artists from the overseas market and putting it into Excel documents to track the weekly sales, both physical and digital ones. This included all international markets, from Argentina to Japan, the United Kingdom, and even countries like the Czech

Republic. There's a ton of sensitive sales numbers on how well an album or single sold, so I had to keep the Excel documents organized and be super detail-oriented to make sure I was inputting the correct numbers in the correct places. I was constantly double-checking my work, trying to be efficient without jeopardizing the quality of the work.

At the end of the week, I sent the collected sales data for an artist to their band manager, which involved sending a lot of emails to important people in the music industry. This required great attention to detail, since the emails contained highly sensitive information about artists and their sales. I had to ensure the emails and Excel documents were sent out without any mistakes.

My other responsibilities included handling the phones, scheduling, scanning, making copies, and shipping…pretty much all administrative duties. I attended meetings and took notes where people discussed how to market artists such as Michael Bublé.

I facilitated phoners, which are interviews between an artist like Green Day with a media outlet like a magazine company from Tokyo. This meant I had to learn how to be stern and professional without coming off in a negative way. I had to be aware of the artist's time and make sure the interviews were kept on schedule and ran smoothly.

As it was such a fast-paced environment, I was given lots of tasks throughout the day. I had to learn to multitask, prioritize, and be a self-starter. It was tough.

Oh, and I also got to take care of Bella Bublé, a dog given to one of my supervisors from Michael Bublé himself!

Q: WAS THIS WHY I SWITCHED TO THE ANIMATION INDUSTRY?

Yes and no. After my WBR internship, my plan was to go back to school and finish my last two quarters, so I could graduate. However, during my internship at WBR, I would drive around Burbank and see the Nickelodeon building. It brought back incredible childhood memories and I thought it would be awesome if I could intern there. In one of my supervisor's offices, there was a Nickelodeon blimp that I saw every day, which I took as a sign to apply to Nickelodeon. I thought I'd give it a shot. It turned out that as an entertainment intern, it's pretty easy to switch industries—as long as you have a major entertainment studio on your resume. It actually makes you more interesting! All in all, I'm still interested in the music industry, but I found greater success in animation.

Q: HOW DID I LAND THE INTERNSHIP AT NICKELODEON ANIMATION STUDIO? WHAT DID I DO?

I applied to Nickelodeon during my internship at WBR and got an interview. I went through a phone interview, an in-person interview, then a few weeks later, I got an offer. This time, I didn't have to buy a plane ticket since I was already in the area.

At Nickelodeon, I was a Vault Intern in the post-production department, where I helped organize and update assets from the golden age of Nickelodeon. I got to see and handle a ton of old stuff such as Rugrat cels, Invader Zim scripts, and the pilot of Hey Arnold, which was a physical reel. It was a truly unique internship position that I wouldn't trade for any other position out there.

Q: WHAT WAS THE APPLICATION AND INTERVIEW PROCESS LIKE?

The application process was simple. I just had to email them with my top three position choices and attach a copy of my resume and cover letter (this process is explained on their website).

In the interview process, there was a phone interview first conducted by the HR intern. They asked me basic questions, such as "Why do you want to intern at Nickelodeon?" The call lasted about 15-20 minutes. If the call goes well, then there's an in-person interview for a specific department. My in-person interview lasted around 45 minutes. They asked me all sorts of difficult questions, and also and silly questions such as "If you could be any salad dressing, what would you be?"

I answered, "I couldn't tell you, because I don't like salad dressing!" They laughed and said it was the most unique answer to that question that they'd heard.

Q: WHAT SET MY APPLICATION APART FROM OTHERS?

Without a doubt, having an internship at WBR on my application form set it apart. It showed that I had experience and interest in the entertainment industry, but also that I was curious to explore other entertainment industries. This also set my interview apart. During the in-person interview, we spent probably half of the time talking about the music industry and what the culture was like at WBR.

Q: ANY ADVICE TO STUDENTS APPLYING TO THE NICKELODEON INTERNSHIP PROGRAM?

Keep it professional. Even though it's Nickelodeon, which is fun, remember you are applying to work there and they want to make sure you can actually work! Don't send silly resumes or cover letters with cartoon drawings on it. Just keep it professional.

Q: ANY ADVICE TO STUDENTS WHO JUST GOT ACCEPTED INTO THE INTERNSHIP PROGRAM THAT I WISH I HAD KNOWN?

Treat the internship as if it's the longest interview of your life. Hit the ground running. Really learn as much as you can and absorb everything from day one. The program goes by fast. Make friends, share experiences, and enjoy it.

Q: HOW WAS THE INTERNSHIP EXPERIENCE OVERALL?

Nickelodeon was ranked as a top 10 internship by Forbes for a reason. It was the best internship that I've ever had, and I still miss it today. Everyone was super friendly, the culture was positive and encouraging, and we even had access to the Paramount Studio to watch free movies! How can you beat that!

Q: WHAT WAS THE BEST PART ABOUT BEING A NICKTERN?

The ping pong tables!

Q: WHAT HAPPENED AFTER THE NICKELODEON INTERNSHIP?

After Nickelodeon, I scored an internship with DreamWorks, where I worked as a Production Intern on the movie Penguins of Madagascar. I assisted multiple departments including art, story, and editorial.

I helped the Production Assistant by providing administrative support, such as taking the absentee list, scheduling, photocopying, printing scripts, and more. I also helped update dialogue scripts and sequences, and organized and updated the art department's digital files through a system called metadata.

I helped with the vendors, food service, and catering for the crew as well. This included taking a head count, ordering, picking up, setting up, labeling the vegetarian meals, announcing when the food was ready, and cleaning up.

The two internships, Nickelodeon and DreamWorks, were totally different, both in terms of the positions and formats. DreamWorks was in movies and Nickelodeon was in TV, and they were in different departments (production vs. post-production).

Q: WHAT WAS THE APPLICATION AND INTERVIEW PROCESS LIKE AT DREAMWORKS?

The application process was simple. I just had to send my cover letter and resume to an email address, with the internship position as the subject line.

The interview process was standard. First, there was a phone screener, then an in-person interview. Since I was going for a production internship, my in-person interview was three back to back interviews for three different productions. A week later, they let me know which production I was accepted for.

Q: WHAT SET MY APPLICATION APART FROM OTHERS?

Having work experience at WBR and Nickelodeon on my resume helped set me apart. Although my experience was in the music industry and in a non-relevant position (Vault intern), it showed that I had experience, was interested in the entertainment industry, and wanted to pursue animation.

Q: ANY ADVICE TO STUDENTS APPLYING TO THE DREAMWORKS INTERNSHIP PROGRAM?

There's a ton of cool departments that they let you intern for. I'd apply to the unique ones. I think they're less impacted and can lead to cool, unique careers.

Work hard, but have fun. The internship supervisors would say "This internship is the longest job interview of your life." So every day, you have to bring it, but you should also balance some fun into it as well. You're competing with yourself, not against the other interns, so don't sabotage your co-interns thinking you'll get ahead. That isn't how it works. Become friends and enjoy the process together. You never know who they'll become later on in their career.

The Animated Shorts Program started as an open submission where anyone, employee or not, could pitch a cartoon idea to Nickelodeon. I thought it would be cool to say that I pitched a cartoon to Nickelodeon during my internship, not really thinking anything would come from it. However, I had never pitched or written a script in my life before, and I was still in college at time.

Right before my pitch meeting, I was rushing because I forgot to fill out the release forms, and I was a mess. When I went in, I could tell they were tired. Mary Harrington, the co-founder of Nickelodeon Animation and executive producer on the animation shorts, listened to the pitches along with another development executive. Mary later confessed that she thought, "Oh, another intern," and when I said I was in the vault department, they were like "Oh great…"

Not to mention, I had no idea how to pitch something, so I was so nervous. As I read it in my monotone voice, they started laughing (at the script - not at me). After the pitch, they loved it so much that my short was pushed up the ladder—and reached executive level. They ultimately passed on it for whatever reason, and it would have been cool if I had got my short made.

However, all was not over, because the following year, after college graduation, Nickelodeon asked whether I could pitch again. I was just going to pitch my old script and spice it up, and I was working on another short that I couldn't quite figure out. Then, the week of the pitch, I got an idea. I sat at my computer and an hour later, *The Outsiders* was born. This short was accepted and very little was changed from the script. It was an out of body experience for me.

Q: WHAT WAS THE EXPERIENCE LIKE?

It was the best experience ever! At the time, unfortunately, I was back at home in the bay and I was looking for a job. I eventually got a job at Google on the Self-Driving Car project, so I was balancing the two. I woke up at 5:30 every morning, took the 6:00am shuttle bus to Google, worked from 7:00am-4:00pm. On the way home, I'd work on *The Outsiders* on the bus, taking phone calls from LA, and replying to various emails from my directors and team. Once I got home, I would eat something light, then head to karate from 7:00-8:00pm. After that, I would go home and eat a proper dinner, work on *The Outsiders* a bit more, then go to sleep. At times, Nickelodeon would fly me down to the studio in Burbank. It was a crazy time, but the best.

Q: WHAT ARE THE CULTURAL DIFFERENCES BETWEEN THE THREE MAJOR STUDIOS NICKELODEON, DREAMWORKS, AND WARNER BROS. RECORDS?

Nickelodeon was super fun! It was my childhood dream fulfilled. The people there really had the "work hard, play hard" motto down.

DreamWorks was a bit more structured for me. I was in the now closed PDI office in Redwood City, away from the awesome Glendale campus. It was definitely a more straightforward internship.

WBR was the most intense. The culture in the music industry is so fast-paced, but it taught me a lot.

Q: WHERE DO I HOPE TO BE IN 5 YEARS?

In five years, I hope to have a cartoon series.

Q: WHAT IS MY DREAM PROJECT?

My dream project was to start my own animation studio, which I've actually just started! It's called Bravo Bros. Studio. We are currently producing an animated short.

Q: WHAT HAS BEEN MY PROUDEST MOMENT SO FAR?

Writing this book. I really do hope it helps people get into animation, so they can do great things!

Q: WHAT'S THE BEST ADVICE I CAN GIVE MY PAST SELF, KNOWING WHAT I KNOW NOW?

If you leave the industry, you have to work your ass off, double time, to get back in. So stay in it!

Q: FAVORITE ANIMATED FILM AND/OR TV SHOW?

Toy Story, Lion King, Ratatouille, Hey Arnold, Regular Show, BoJack Horseman, Rick & Morty.

Q: SOME WORK I'D LIKE TO SHARE:

Personal Website: www.eric-bravo.com

Travel Blog: www.letsgobravo.com

Studio: www.bravobrosstudio.com

CHAPTER 1

Starting Out

Understanding The World Of Animation

There seems to be a myth that in order to work in animation, you need to be able to draw. I'm here to set the record straight. While drawing may help you get an artist position or get into a trainee program, most internship programs in animation are performing administrative work, gearing you up to become an assistant. So, you don't need to be able to draw to be in animation. Pretty neat, huh?

In this chapter, I'll introduce you to the general world of internships in animation. I'll go over the required qualifications to become an intern, tell you whether or not having an animation or film degree matters, and give you an overview of the available internship positions that these programs offer, along with a brief description for each department. Let's begin!

INTERNSHIP QUALIFICATIONS

The internship requirements vary from studio to studio. The information in this section is the general qualifications that most studios require in order to become an intern. However, to be completely certain of the qualifications and requirements for each internship program, make sure to check the specific studio's internship web page by doing a quick Google search. There, you'll find the studio's most up-to-date qualifications and requirements.

YOU MUST BE A COLLEGE STUDENT

There are no high school internships. You must be a college student to be an intern and you must be enrolled in an accredited four year degree-granting university or college.

RECENT GRADUATES CAN APPLY TOO

Some studios offer internships to students who have graduated within six months from the start of the internship, and others offer up to one year from graduation. The exception is Walt Disney Animation. They have a program called the Apprenticeship, designed for recent college graduates who graduate within three years from the start of the program.

THE SEMESTER SYSTEM

All internships are on a semester system, meaning that they only have internship programs during Fall (September - December), Spring (February - May), and Summer (June - August) semesters.

If you are in the quarter system at school, like I was, you have to work around the semester system. Fall internships for quarter students don't cause any problems since most universities break for the holidays. However, Spring internships are where things can get a bit difficult. This applies mainly to those students who don't live close to the studios.

I had a problem with my Spring internship at Nickelodeon. It started a month after my school's Winter quarter began and ended mid-way through my Spring quarter. I knew this was going to be a problem because it would overlap two quarters, and I didn't want to take two full quarters off school.

During my interview, I was honest and explained that if I were given the opportunity, I would have to leave mid- internship to return to school. I took the risk of jeopardizing my acceptance at Nickelodeon. With some luck, the department I was interviewing for was very accommodating and allowed me to leave early.

Spring internships for quarter students can be a delicate situation. Not all departments will be so nice, so be wary when applying.

HOW LONG ARE INTERNSHIPS?

Internships range between 10-12 weeks. Some programs allow you to stay longer or begin earlier.

CAN YOU RETURN AS AN INTERN?

This is dependent on how well you did, and whether the program allows it. For example, DreamWorks allows you to return as an intern, even in the same department.

YOU NEED TO PROVIDE A SCHOOL LETTER

Once accepted, you'll need to provide the studio with a letter from your school confirming that you are in fact a college student attending their college or university. This letter must have your school's letterhead on it.

WHAT'S THE DIFFERENCE BETWEEN GETTING SCHOOL CREDIT VS. BEING PAID?

If the internship doesn't pay, you'll be required to accept school credit. If you're a senior and have financial aid or are on a scholarship, you should double-check to make sure you don't go over your allotted credits.

If it's a paid internship, then you don't need to receive school credit. How much you get paid is dependent on the studio.

ARE HOUSING AND TRANSPORTATION PROVIDED?

Most, if not all, internships don't offer housing or transportation, even for those coming from outside the area.

If your internship requires you to drive, be sure to ask for gas reimbursement.

ARE THERE RESIDENCY PROGRAMS?

A residency program is when a studio invites students (usually graduate students) to become full-time employees for up to a year or two.

These are not typical internships. They are usually in the Technical Direction and Software Research and Development departments. Pixar offers residencies of up to one year for these types of programs.

WHAT ARE THE WORK DAYS AND HOURS LIKE?

You'll need to work at least 16 hour a week (two full 8-hour days), but no more than 35 hours per week. On average, you'll be working 15-20 hours per week depending on the studio and your position.

During my internship at DreamWorks, my department was strict in only allowing me to work two days per week. However, I know other interns in other departments that were allowed to work four days per week.

At Warner Bros. and Nickelodeon, I was allowed to and did work four full days per week.

YOU NEED TO PROVIDE WORK AUTHORIZATION

You need to be able to work in the United States for these internships.

For student visa applicants, you must contact your international student advisor to make sure you can qualify.

ARE THERE PERKS?

Each program offers perks, such as resume classes, invitations to company events, and amenities such as movie screenings and guest lectures. At DreamWorks, there's free food and movie giveaways. At Nickelodeon, there was a soda machine and free cereal. The perks differ at each studio.

DO I NEED A PORTFOLIO OR REEL?

You'll only need this if you are applying to a specific trainee program dealing with software and technology or artist roles that require a learned skill. For general internships in animation, a portfolio or reel is not required.

PICK A MAJOR, ANY MAJOR!

In general, recruiters don't care whether you are majoring in engineering, business, film, or double majoring in computer science and Japanese. The internship may say certain majors are preferred, but it is not a requirement. Students with any major can get an animation internship.

What the recruiters are looking for is your interest in entertainment. That's it. They want to see how passionate and enthusiastic you are about the entertainment field and if you are majoring in animation or film, that's even better.

I majored in Managerial Economics and let's just say I know way more about agricultural trackers and running a farm than I'd ever thought I would. I've never taken an animation class and I ended up with two animation internships and a cartoon under my belt. The crazy part is, I can't even draw! If you're majoring in animation, great! If you aren't, but have a strong interest in it, don't be afraid to apply.

Types Of Internship Roles

Here you'll find a list of common positions you might find at an animation studio. I'll describe the departments a bit more than the responsibilities of an intern, since the responsibilities of animation internships mostly consist of administrative work. Most internships in animation aren't artistic, so I won't be touching on artistic roles here.

INTERN RESPONSIBILITIES:

Depending on what department you're working for, you will have different work assignments. However, most interns will have admin work, such as assisting your supervisor with their daily tasks.

PRODUCTION INTERN

The production internship is part of the production pipeline. It's one of the most sought-out internships in animation. As a Production Intern, you'll be assigned to work on a TV show or movie, then assigned to a specific department within it. The departments can range from art to story, editorial, lighting and effects, etc. Your goal is to be the friendly, approachable face of the production team, offering and anticipating help to anyone and everyone.

Your tasks can include scanning, making photocopies, shipping, handling phones, e-mailing, and scheduling. Other duties include booking meeting rooms, dealing with vendors, and handling food service and catering for the crew. You might also attend daily meetings where you help set up, take notes, and clean up.

DEVELOPMENT INTERN

The Development Intern is part of the development team. The team finds original ideas and tries to develop them to become a TV series or movie.

ARCHIVE & RESOURCE LIBRARY

The Archive & Resource Library Intern is part of the Vault department, which is responsible for updating and organizing various assets, such as background paintings, old cels from TV shows or movies, scripts, etc. The intern's main job is to help keep the library up to date and current.

CASTING

The Casting Intern works in the casting department. This group finds and auditions talent for various productions. This intern requires very strong interpersonal skills and good oral communication.

FINANCE

The Finance Intern works in the finance department. This intern works more on the corporate side and helps with anything related to budgets, such as production costs or staff wages.

HUMAN RESOURCES

The HR Intern works in the HR department, which finds, reaches out, reviews, and interviews potential employees or talent for open positions. This intern requires very strong interpersonal skills.

MUSIC

The Music Intern works in the music department, helping with voice recording session and follies.

POST-PRODUCTION

The Post Production Intern works in the post-production department, which deals with editing the production and getting it ready for release. This is a faster-paced environment with lots of deadlines for the intern to juggle.

PRESS & COMMUNICATIONS

The Press & Communications Intern is in the press and communications department dealing with the public. This department is the liaison between the studio and the media.

SOCIAL MEDIA

The Social Media Intern helps manage the social media accounts for the studio. Great creative writing skills are helpful here.

MARKETING

The Marketing Intern is part of the marketing department, helping to market various studio assets.

SPECIAL EVENTS

Also under the marketing umbrella, this intern helps plan, organize, and execute any events held by the company, from a TV/movie premiere to a cast holiday party.

Building Experience

Internships are meant to give you experience to help build your resume. However, entertainment internships are a bit different in that they want you to have some prior entertainment experience before applying. Ah-ha, our first catch 22! In order to get over this hump and to better your chances of hopping on board one of these ships, you'll have to plan ahead. Way ahead!

HOW TO STAND OUT WHEN APPLYING

The easiest way to stand out is to be **open-minded**. One trick I learned when applying to entertainment internships, is that you should never limit yourself to just one industry or department. I hear you saying, "But this book is dedicated to animation!" Hear me out first.

In the back of my mind, I always knew I wanted to intern at Nickelodeon, but I also knew it wasn't going to be a direct shot. The only reason I was able to become a Nicktern was because I had just interned at Warner Bros. Records (WBR), a very well-known studio name. During my in-person interview at Nick, they were so interested in what I did at WBR that we spent half of the interview chatting about the culture there and the music industry.

So, if you know you want to do animation and you're not getting interviews from any studios, why not apply to music or live-action companies instead? For your first internship, your goal is to work at any major, well-known studio, no matter the industry. After this, the flood gates will open—trust me. At an intern level, they understand you are still testing the waters, exploring your career options, and recruiters are more lenient if you are switching industries. If anything, a different industry makes you and your resume stand out more. But that doesn't mean you should stop applying to animation studios either! Still apply at every chance you get. I'm just suggesting that you expand your search across multiple industries.

In addition, the knowledge and skills you develop at any internship are transferable, meaning you can apply them to your next one. The skills and knowledge that I gained from my International Marketing Internship at WBR was far more useful in my career than what I learned at Nickelodeon or DreamWorks. It really set a solid foundation for me, being that it was in the fast-paced, cut-throat environment of the music industry. I'm not saying the other studios had bad internships, in fact, the Nickelodeon internship was the absolute best and by far my favorite. But the skills I learned at WBR were so much more valuable that I still use them today.

Once you have a major studio on your resume, no matter what industry it is in, it will open more doors and help you land an internship at your desired studio. The bottom line is, be open-minded when starting your search into animation and consider applying to other entertainment industries as well.

Who knows, you might like an industry you never thought of trying. Remember, it doesn't matter at an internship level what industry you're in. If your end goal is animation, you'll get there eventually. You just need a break in —and the break can come from any industry.

HOW TO GAIN EXPERIENCE FOR YOUR RESUME

The first step on your journey to an animation internship is getting relevant experience to put on your resume. How might you get relevant experience you ask? Well, join a club or organization on campus and get a leadership position. It's as simple as that. It should be a club related to animation, anime, film, or entertainment in general, whatever your interests are. Being a member is good, and you can definitely put that on your resume and explain what you do, but in order to show more, you want to be more active by holding a titled position in the club. Once you join, see whether you can get a position such as president, treasurer, or secretary, etc. If there are no clubs that you like, or no organizations related to animation at your school, start one! I guarantee this will be a plus for your resume.

For example, prior to animation, I really wanted to get into the music industry, but I had no experience in the music industry. Regardless, I applied to various music companies' internship programs. With little surprise, I heard nothing from any of them. My resume during that period consisted of my time at Re/Max Gold (a real estate internship), Videographer for a non-profit, and my college business fraternity experience.

I knew I had to show that I was interested in music more than the mere fact that I liked to listen to music. I had to prove that I was interested in the music industry and I was doing something related to it. So, I ended up volunteering for KDVS, UC Davis' radio station. With this addition to my resume, it proved that I liked music more than the average Joe and that I was involved in something music-related. This made all the difference when I applied for the Fall internship program again. This time, I only applied to WBR and I landed three interviews in different departments all for the Fall quarter. You need to apply this same logic to the animation studios that you're applying to. The power of **relevant experience** is no joke.

Q & A With Garrett Prince

- Project Manager & Part-Time Designer, Black Ops at Dropbox
- Global Production Supervisor, Image Finaling at DreamWorks Animation
- Production Coordinator at DreamWorks Animation
- Producer's Assistant/Central Coordinator at DreamWorks Animation
- Production Assistant at DreamWorks Animation
- Production Assistant on *Winnie the Pooh* at Walt Disney Animation Studios
- Production Intern on *The Mighty B!* at Nickelodeon Animation Studios
- Nickelodeon Writing Fellowship Awards & Festivals at Nickelodeon Animation Studios

Starting off as an intern at Nickelodeon Animation Studios in the Writing Fellowship department, Garrett Prince quickly transitioned into the world of animation and has steadily climbed the Production ladder. He has worked on various shows and feature films including, Nickelodeon's *The Mighty B!* and Walt Disney's *Winnie the Pooh*.

Since graduating from Chapman University with a degree in Public Relations & Advertising, Garrett has worked at three major animation studios, including Walt Disney Animation Studios, Nickelodeon Animation Studio, and DreamWorks Animation Studios.

Update: Since this interview, Garrett is currently working at Dropbox as a Project Manager and part-time Designer.

Q: AS A GLOBAL PRODUCTION SUPERVISOR, WHAT DO YOU DO?

I am a creative wrangler. Working as a Global Production Supervisor for the Image Finaling Department at DreamWorks Animation, I strategize, organize, and maintain balance among artists within the exciting, and often chaotic, atmosphere of animation.

Q: WHAT COLLEGE DID YOU ATTEND AND WHAT WAS YOUR MAJOR? DO YOU THINK THIS HELPED WITH YOUR PURSUIT IN THE ENTERTAINMENT INDUSTRY?

I attended Chapman University, where I majored in Public Relations & Advertising. I would say this major helped in a very peripheral way. During a class lecture, the Director of Nickelodeon's Writing Fellowship program came to speak. She became my initial contact and future mentor within the entertainment industry.

Q: WHEN DID YOU KNOW YOU WANTED TO BE IN THE ENTERTAINMENT/ANIMATION INDUSTRY AND WHAT EVENTS LED YOU TO CHOOSE IT?

I always loved cartoons growing up, specifically *The Ren & Stimpy Show*. I never thought I would enter this as a career. It was only when I began my internship at Nickelodeon that I got my first taste for the industry and for production work. I immediately gravitated towards the work, and the career path developed from there.

Q: DID ANYONE/ANYTHING INSPIRE YOU TO FOLLOW YOUR PASSION FOR ENTERTAINMENT?

My first mentor in the field was Karen Kirkland (currently VP of Talent Development & Outreach at Nickelodeon Animation Studio). I interned for Karen when she was the Director of Writing & Artist Programs at Nickelodeon. It was her career and advice that truly set my course within the industry.

Q: HOW DID YOU LAND THE NICKELODEON WRITING FELLOWSHIP & FESTIVALS INTERNSHIP AT NICKELODEON? WHAT DID YOU DO THERE?

Timing and persistence. This industry is extremely competitive and I would encourage anyone looking to work in entertainment to build genuine relationships and always be passionate about any opportunities that arise. With Nickelodeon in particular, I approached Karen Kirkland directly after her talk at my school and asked her about internship opportunities, which happened to be right when she was hiring. In the Writing Fellowship Program, I did a variety of intern tasks, including archiving, script coverage, and festival packet preparation. This was really my sponge phase. I absorbed so much during the internship that forced me to lend a hand wherever I could and gain a better understanding of the industry and what role I could potentially serve.

Q: WHAT WAS THE APPLICATION AND INTERVIEW PROCESS LIKE? WHAT DO YOU THINK SET YOUR APPLICATION/INTERVIEW APART FROM OTHERS?

It's hard to say what set my application apart. I would imagine it actually looked quite similar to others who were applying.

At this stage, since experience is limited, it's important to make sure your resume reads clearly and includes at least some job experience that showcases a work ethic. What I hope set my application apart was my on-site interview. I remember that I was very eager and excited about this potential opportunity and held it in the highest regard. I loved that internship; it helped build my foundation for where I am.

Q: FROM NICKELODEON WRITING FELLOWSHIP & FESTIVAL DEPARTMENT, YOU MOVED ONTO *THE MIGHTY B!* — HOW WAS THAT?

It was fantastic! The crew on the project was amazing. It was my first experience in a more production-related path, handling similar tasks that may normally have been required of a Production Assistant.

Q: ANY ADVICE TO STUDENTS APPLYING TO THE NICKELODEON INTERNSHIP PROGRAM?

Definitely apply! If you don't have the opportunity initially, these roles are all about timing, and the more you pursue these opportunities, the better chances you have of landing something.

Q: ANY ADVICE TO STUDENTS WHO JUST GOT ACCEPTED INTO THE INTERNSHIP PROGRAM THAT YOU WISH YOU HAD KNOWN?

It may sound cliché, but the internship goes very quickly. I didn't realize it at the time, but the skills I was learning and the people I was meeting would continue to shape my career. My advice would be to really make the most of any time you have there.

Everything I was able to get involved in at Nick didn't disappoint. Nickelodeon is a very special place. The best part about being a Nicktern is being involved in a place and process that has been entertainment for so many people growing up. Being around this environment and process was a constant reminder of how important the art form is.

Q: AFTER YOUR TIME AT NICKELODEON, YOU SCORED A PRODUCTION ASSISTANT POSITION AT WALT DISNEY ANIMATION STUDIOS. WHAT WAS THAT LIKE?

I'm lucky to have worked at Disney, especially on the staff of *Winnie the Pooh*. The film housed the careers of so many talented 2D animators who were responsible for many prior Disney classics. The film contained so much talent and was a unique interpretation of a familiar story. I assisted the animators and production staff directly, driving dailies and ensuring proper tracking and stamping with every hand-drawn frame and shot. It was my first feature film experience and an opportunity to work with some amazing legends in the field. I will never forget that experience.

Q: AFTER YOUR TIME AT WALT DISNEY ANIMATION, YOU SCORED A PRODUCER ASSISTANT/CENTRAL COORDINATOR POSITION WITH DREAMWORKS ANIMATION STUDIOS. WHAT DID YOU DO THERE?

As a Production Assistant, I was the link between the producer and several key points of contact on the feature. In addition to traditional Producer Assistant responsibilities (scheduling, answering phones, booking travel, etc.), it was my job to ensure the consistency and accuracy of all information that the producer needed. A producer's time is extremely valuable, and I was the gatekeeper. I paired this role with the Central Coordinator for the show, where I helped set up and maintain the show calendar, incorporating the show's numerous production meetings.

Q: IS THERE A DIFFERENCE BETWEEN THE ROLES OF A PRODUCTION ASSISTANT AND A PRODUCER ASSISTANT? AS A PRODUCTION COORDINATOR AT DREAMWORKS, WHAT WERE YOUR DAILY TASKS?

As a Production Assistant, you're far more involved in the production process. In my PA roles, I had the opportunity to drive dailies, and work with

Production Coordinators and Supervisors to resolve schedule conflicts and address deadlines. I had far more interaction with the artists on the films as well. These skills were extremely valuable as I made my transition to Production Coordinator. Daily tasks for a Production Coordinator are highly involved.

You're the direct link to the Production Supervisor and maintain the updated information from daily check-ins with the artists on your team; information that is sought from you often. I saw the Production Coordinator role very much as a Production Supervisor in training role. I maintained a tracker and worked to take over several responsibilities. In this position, you have the opportunity to take on more because you've built up trust as a Production Assistant. This is your time to learn more about the production process, but also gain experience without being fully responsible for the team, like you are in the Supervisor position. I learned the most as a Coordinator for a variety of departments.

Q: USUALLY AFTER BEING A PRODUCTION COORDINATOR, THE NEXT STEP IS BECOMING A PRODUCTION MANAGER, BUT YOU ENDED UP TAKING A DIFFERENT PATH. NOW, YOU ARE A GLOBAL PRODUCTION SUPERVISOR, IMAGE FINALING AT DREAMWORKS. WHY DID YOU DECIDE TO GO THIS PATH AND HOW?

A Production Coordinator would normally shoot for a Production Supervisor role next. This role adds more responsibility and Production Manager interaction, but also focuses on a people/team management component, which you wouldn't have with the Coordinator role. I chose this department path because Image Finaling was not only unique to DreamWorks, it was unique to the Redwood City studio specifically. Since this department handles requests from all projects, including marketing, I saw it as an amazing opportunity for growth and experience.

Q: WHAT DO YOU DO AS A GLOBAL PRODUCTION SUPERVISOR AND WHAT DOES YOUR DAY-TO-DAY LOOK LIKE? ANY ADVICE FOR SOMEONE WHO MIGHT BE INTERESTED IN PURSUING A POSITION LIKE THIS?

Production Supervisor role is an incredible macro view of what's involved in a feature film. As a supervisor for the Image Finaling department, I strategize the workflow and schedule for every feature, short, and marketing component that may hit our department. I work with production managers, studio executives, and marketing heads to determine staffing, shot deadlines, and long-term projections. My day-to- day consists of maintaining artist priorities, implementing project deadlines, and weekly reporting to continue the success of our department and goals. It's important that I stay aware of any changes or report any potential concerns. If anyone has an opportunity to take this route, I would highly recommend it. Working in the department expanded my interactions within the studio, but also gave me an insane amount of context for what is involved in our filmmaking.

I also had the opportunity to work with our India studio on two features, which was a huge plus.

Q: HAVING WORKED AT THE PDI/DREAMWORKS OFFICE FOR SEVERAL YEARS, HOW DO YOU FEEL ABOUT IT SHUTTING DOWN?

It was a devastating experience. Many of the people who worked there I consider as family. Whether we worked on projects together, ate lunch together, or passed each other in the halls, PDI was an incredible group of talent and hard-working individuals who all gave many hours of their lives to that studio. The only positive thing about the closure was the fact that it solidified how truly important everyone was to each other and how much we cared about the same things.

Q: WHAT ARE THE CULTURAL DIFFERENCES BETWEEN THE THREE MAJOR ANIMATION STUDIOS YOU HAVE WORKED AT: NICKELODEON, WALT DISNEY, AND DREAMWORKS?

The cultural experiences at each studio were similar in the sense that everyone involved in a production cared about the end goal, not only for the team they were on, but for the project as a whole. I was at DreamWorks the longest and had the most experience in a variety of roles there, so it's hard to compare all three evenly. However, having been involved with the other studios in different capacities, I can say that the sense of community and friendship is consistent. I'm still in touch with people from all three studios, and the fun and crazy experiences one shares when involved in making a film are present at all three.

CHAPTER 2

Preparing Your Resume

How To Write A Resume

When applying to an internship, your resume is the company's first look at you, so you want it to be the best it can be. Many people believe that since they are applying to a creative company, they need to get creative with their resume. This is not the case. I've heard horror stories from recruiters about students getting too creative, like someone who thought it was a good idea to send a jack in the box! The recruiter opened it and the resume smacked her right in the face. This is a definite no. Another student sent a package with glitter all over her resume. The recruiter opened it and made a huge mess. The recruiter had to clean it up and was not particularly happy about it. I think we all know why she didn't get a call back.

With that being said, this doesn't mean you can't add hints of creativity in your resume while also keeping it professional. In my current resume, I added a bit of subtle creativity in the bullet points. Potential employees and recruiters might see this as being detailed-oriented, and it demonstrates creativity and uniqueness. Here are five major things to remember when crafting your resume.

1. MAKE IT PROFESSIONAL

Send a professional resume. The company wants to know that you are professional and will treat the internship as such. For example, a Pixar employee informed me that the people at Pixar are a little type-A: ambitious, highly organized, striving for perfection, so there shouldn't be any misspellings in your resume—as a typo can affect a call back.

2. TAILOR YOUR RESUME

For whatever position you apply to, make sure you tailor your resume to that specific role. Read the job description over and over again to apply your prior experience to what they are asking for. One of Pixar's recruiters informed me that if you're applying to a Marketing Internship role, you have to show that you are interested in marketing by having experience in marketing. Tailor your resume to marketing and take out what doesn't belong.

If you followed the previous chapter, you should have this one covered as you have gained relevant experience to add to your resume.

If you are sending a general resume for any position, tailor your resume to the industry.

3. KEEP TO ONE PAGE

This is probably the hardest thing to do on a resume. You want to say everything that you did, but you need to choose the right phrases. Since you are in college, you probably don't have a ton of work experience. But if you do, I'd strongly recommend sticking to one page only. I still keep mine to one page. It makes it look clean and forces you to carefully construct your bullet points.

4. EXPORT PDF ONLY

Always remember to export your document to a PDF format. This is standard practice and makes your resume look nice and clean.

5. REREAD YOUR RESUME

After you export it, go over it to make sure everything came out perfectly and that there are no mistakes. Look for typos, punctuation, formatting, and grammatical errors. You should also have someone else review it, as an extra set of eyes is helpful.

MY CURRENT RESUME

This is my most current resume. I am constantly improving the design and bullet points with each job that I apply to. As you go through my resume history in this chapter, you'll see some major differences, especially in design. I believe a good balance of content and design will make any recruiter want to speak with you, because you've put in the effort to make your resume stand out.

ERIC BRAVO

EDUCATION

Bachelor of Science
Managerial Economics

University of California, Davis
2010 - 2013

SKILLS

Photoshop

Adobe Suite CC

MS Office

Gmail/Outlook

Mac/PC Proficient

Final Cut Pro

FileMaker Pro

CONTACT

555-555-5555

www.eric-bravo.com

youremail@gmail.com

Experience

Google[X] Self-Driving Car · Mountain View, CA · Jan 2015 · April 2016
Mapping Operations Associate

- Managed multiple projects to ensure all dynamic deadlines were met and completed with detailed accuracy
- Responsible for tracking and responding to high priority data request
- Created, tested, and maintained detailed maps for Google's Self-Driving Car Project
- Used analytical skills to find improvements in the map building tools and processes
- Created efficiencies of crucial component for the self-driving car technology using proprietary software
- Developed, updated, and maintained internal wiki pages, guides, and manuals for software training making sure it was clear, concise, and accurate.

Nickelodeon Animation Studios · Burbank, CA · April 2014 · April 2016
Creator & Writer

- Created a 2-minute cartoon short as part of Nickelodeon Animated Shorts Program 2014
- Developed original characters and wrote a character driven script
- Oversaw each stage of development and was involved in the creative input from development to completion
- Maintained a production schedule and workflow to ensure all deadlines and goals were met
- Actively communicated across teams to drive the development process

DreamWorks Animation Studios · Redwood City, CA · Sept 2013 · Dec 2013
Production Intern

- Administrative support for production staff including data entry, scheduling, event planning, deliveries, errands, food service and catering set up
- Updated sequences, dialogue scripts and story layouts for the feature film Penguins of Madagascar
- Communicated with the overseas studio and other departments regarding schedules, notes, and any issues they may have
- Assisted the art, editorial and story departments ensuring that all requests were met on time
- Organized the art department's digital art files by naming and categorizing each item in the studio's internal database
- Planned several office events and decorated the production offices to create a friendly and supportive atmosphere

Nickelodeon Animation Studios · Burbank, CA · Feb 2013 · April 2013
Post Production & Vault Intern

- Used FileMaker Pro to archive and document recently aired shows and other assets to keep the vault current
- Labeled and documented overseas assets into the library database at the offsite facility
- Prepared and backed up ProTools sessions discs from various Nickelodeon productions for digital storage

Warner Bros. Records · Burbank, CA · Sept 2012 · Dec 2012
International Marketing Intern

- Facilitated publicity and promotional phone interviews between artists and foreign media
- Used Excel to maintain current sales data to track the progress of every artist under Warner Bros. Records in all foreign countries on a daily basis
- Created and sent weekly management reports of the overseas sales to band managers
- Performed administrative tasks, such as data entry, handling phones, scheduling, e-mailing, note-taking, scanning and making copies
- Took notes in marketing meetings discussing marketing strategies for current and upcoming projects

STRUCTURING YOUR RESUME

Your resume should consist of:

- Your contact information

- Name (should be capitalized, bolded, and in a bigger font)

- E-mail

- Phone number

- Address (optional) – Lately, I've been leaving my address out. I have been applying to jobs across the country and I don't want the recruiters to pass on my resume just because I don't live close by.

- Website (optional) – Only add a website if it is directly related to the job's skills/qualification that you are applying for. If you have very little experience in animation, but you have a collection of your work displayed on your website, add it. It'll show your interest in animation.

RELATED WORK EXPERIENCE

- Arrange your experience in reverse chronologic order with your latest work experience at the top. Be sure to include volunteer and non-paid work as well if it's relevant.

- Include the company's name, location, duration of employment (month and year), and the title of your position.

- Add bullet points to explain your responsibilities and accomplishments using phrases. You'll want to use phrases instead of full sentences. Don't use or begin with "I." Try to use action works such as managed, administrated, led, organized, analyzed, or responsible for.

- Your current work experience should be in present tense; everything prior should be in past tense.

- If you had similar responsibilities for different roles, try to re-phrase the bullet point, instead of saying the same thing.

EDUCATION

- Include the school you are attending and your current or proposed major and minor.

- Include the year you started and the proposed graduation date.

- Only include your GPA if it is higher than a 3.5.

- If you have any accomplishments, add those too. Accomplishments can be high honors, growing your membership of your animation club, or winning a student film competition.

- Listing classes is not necessary, unless it is for a marketing or finance position where relevant classes will show your knowledge and capability to perform in the position.

SKILLS

- List any particular skills you've used in the work environment or strengths that you can use in the position you're applying for.

- List the skills that are most important to your targeted employers.

- Don't sell yourself short, but don't over exaggerate.

- Look at the job description to find key verbs; speak the same language as they do.

ACTIVITIES

I don't have any activities listed on my current resume; however, I did include them on my college resume within the Skills section. This was because I need to fill my resume with more information. Activities can be any clubs or organizations you belong to. For example, I was part of the student body government and also held a position for my business fraternity. Activities should imply some skills. There are so many resumes that say "reading and sports," which really tells the employer nothing useful.

REVIEWING AND IMPROVING YOUR RESUME

It's important to regularly review your resume to improve it, and keep it up to date with your new skills, experience, and achievements. Now you can take a look through my past resumes. I have listed them in chronological order starting with Warner Bros. Records, Nickelodeon, and then DreamWorks, so you can see the progression.

WARNER BROS. RECORDS RESUME

This is the resume that I sent to Warner Bros. Records. I've reviewed it with my mistakes and the improvements I could have made to it. Obviously, you'll want to model your resume after my current resume; however, it is helpful to review my past mistakes so you can avoid making them on your resume.

Eric Bravo

Phone: (831) 555- 5555 *Email:* myemail@gmail.com

Address: 123 None St. Hollywood, CA

OBJECTIVE

An internship position at Warner Bros. Records utilizing research and analysis, creativity, team-driven success, and leadership in a dynamic learning environment.

EXPERIENCE

90.3 KDVS   *February '12-March '12*
Volunteer
- Updated DJ profile sections on website to keep sections current.
- Maintained and organized the vinyl/CD collection.
- Performed data entry and other administrative duties.

Sacramento Grant A Wish – Sacramento, California   *December '10-February '11*
Marketing Intern
- Developed media outlets and encouraged more traffic though Twitter, YouTube and Facebook.
- Produced promotional videos to illustrate the mission statement and promote upcoming events to potential sponsors and volunteers.
- Worked closely with managers and co-workers to ensure project deadlines were met.

Re/Max Gold – Elk Grove, California   *November '10-February '11*
Intern
- Maintained current data and promoted real estate information and services online though various websites.
- Prepared real estate packages including property descriptions, contract forms and disclosures.
- Assisted realtors with open houses including distributing flyers and communicating with potential clients.

Delta Sigma Pi
Nu Rho Chapter – University of California, Davis   *September '10-Present*
Collegiate Member
- Vice President of Alumni Relations (Winter/Spring 2011) –Liaison between the alumni and chapter members; sent bimonthly alumni email updates, created LinkedIn job posting group; organized and hosted alumni panel during recruitment week; planned alumni social events.

Pi Chi Chapter – University of California, Santa Cruz   *October '09-Present*
Founding Father
- Successfully established Delta Sigma Pi International Professional Fraternity at the University of California, Santa Cruz.
- Collaborated within a group to organize and promote professional and community service events.
- Worked closely with other members to raise money for the colony and to ensure the efficient use of funds.
- Completed various long-term tasks to ensure Delta Sigma Pi's prosperity at University of California, Santa Cruz such as creating the chapter's by-laws, rules and regulations.
- Designed the colony's first T-Shirt to promote recruitment week to potential prospects.

SKILLS/ACTIVITIES

- Computer: Mac/PC literate, proficient in MS Word, MS Excel, MS PowerPoint, Apple's Logic Pro 9, GarageBand, Final Cut Pro and Aperture and fundamental use of Adobe's Photoshop CS5, Illustrator CS5, and Affect Effects CS5.
- Leadership: Delta Sigma Pi - Vice President of Alumni Relations (Winter/Spring 2011). Student Union Assembly Representative (Spring '09). College 10 Senate Member (Jan '09-June'10).
- Work Style: Passionate, motivated, takes initiative, and detail and goal oriented. Keen ability to find new solutions to challenging tasks while using both leadership and collaborative skills.
- Elementary Japanese and Spanish.

EDUCATION

University of California, Davis   *September '10-Present*
    BS in **Management Economics** (Expected Graduation 2012)
University of California, Santa Cruz   *September '08-June '10*

OVERALL DESIGN:

In terms of design, I kept it traditional and professional. I didn't add any eye-popping design to this resume.

CONTACT:

This is a stylized personal choice, but I now capitalize my entire name (like ERIC BRAVO) instead of just using uppercase (Eric Bravo). I believe this draws attention to your name, making it bold and fuller for the recruiter.

OBJECTIVE:

An objective gives the recruiter one sentence explaining why you are applying for the job. However, this isn't necessary if you're providing a cover letter along with your resume. I included an objective on this resume and sent a cover letter as well, but this section isn't found in many resumes today.

EXPERIENCE:

The only relevant music experience I had was volunteering at 90.3 KDVS and the information in the bullet points wasn't that strong. Ideally, you should extend the phrases to reach the far right of the page. Also, don't put "." like I did. They're phrases not sentences. I did apply and got interviews for Marketing, International Marketing, and Video Production. My marketing internship along with the 90.3 volunteer position made it clear that I was interested in music and marketing.

SKILLS/ACTIVITIES:

This section looked kind of messy, but I arranged it by computer skills, leadership skills, my work style, and languages.

EDUCATION:

I transferred from UC Santa Cruz to UC Davis, so I included that. I put my expected graduation date next to my proposed major. I didn't include my GPA because it was bad. The rule of thumb here is: if you have a good GPA, 3.5 or better, then include it. It shows that you are a diligent student. If not, your GPA is not necessary. Entertainment internships don't really care about your GPA, but more about your experience and personality.

There's still a bit of room at the bottom, but that's okay. They understand that you are a college student and probably won't have that much experience on your resume to fill up an entire page. It would look better to increase your line spacing throughout, so there isn't just a big gap at the bottom. Alternatively, you could add to the bullet points with more detail of the work you've done to avoid it looking empty.

NICKELODEON ANIMATION STUDIO RESUME

This is the resume that I sent to Nickelodeon Animation Studio. It was pretty much the same resume as the WBR resume.

Eric Bravo

Phone: (415) 555-5555   *Email:* youremail@gmail.com

Address: 123 None St. Hollywood, CA

OBJECTIVE

Seeking an internship position at Nickelodeon Animation Studios where I can effectively utilize my creativity, research and analysis skills, and leadership in the dynamic learning environment of production within a feature animation studio.

EXPERIENCE

Warner Bros. Records – Burbank, CA   *September '12-Present*
International Marketing Intern
- Maintain current sales data to track the progress of every Warner Bros. Records artist in all foreign countries on a daily basis.
- Facilitate publicity and promotional interviews between artists and foreign media by ensuring interviews are kept on schedule.
- Create and distribute weekly overseas sales reports to band managers.
- Perform administrative tasks, such as data entry, answering the phone, scheduling, e-mailing, scanning and making copies.

Sacramento Grant A Wish – Sacramento, California   *December '10-February '11*
Intern
- Produced promotional videos on Final Cut Pro to illustrate the mission statement and promote upcoming events to potential sponsors and volunteers.
- Developed media outlets and encouraged more traffic though Twitter, YouTube and Facebook.
- Worked closely with managers and co-workers to ensure project deadlines were met.

Re/Max Gold – Elk Grove, California   *November '10-February '11*
Intern
- Maintained current data and promoted real estate information and services online though various websites.
- Prepared real estate packages including property descriptions, contract forms and disclosures.
- Assisted realtors with open houses including distributing flyers and communicating with potential clients.

Delta Sigma Pi
Nu Rho Chapter – University of California, Davis   *September '10-Present*
Collegiate Member
- Vice President of Alumni Relations (Winter/Spring 2011) –Liaison between the alumni and chapter members; sent bimonthly alumni email updates, created LinkedIn job posting group; organized and hosted alumni panel during recruitment week; planned alumni social events.

Pi Chi Chapter – University of California, Santa Cruz   *October '09-Present*
Founding Father
- Successfully established Delta Sigma Pi International Professional Fraternity at the university.
- Collaborated within a group to organize and promote professional and community service events.
- Worked closely with other members to raise money for the colony and to ensure the efficient use of funds.
- Completed various long-term tasks to ensure Delta Sigma Pi's prosperity at the university by creating the chapter's by-laws, rules and regulations.
- Designed the colony's first T-Shirt to promote recruitment week to potential prospects.

SKILLS/ACTIVITIES

- Computer: Mac/PC literate, proficient in MS Word, MS Excel, MS PowerPoint, MS Outlook, Apple's Logic Pro 9, Final Cut Pro and Aperture and fundamental use of Adobe's CS5 Photoshop, Dreamweaver, and Affect Effects.
- Leadership: Delta Sigma Pi - Vice President of Alumni Relations (Winter/Spring 2011). Student Union Assembly Representative (Spring '09). College 10 Senate Member (Jan '09-June'10).
- Work Style: Passionate, motivated, takes initiative, and detail and goal oriented. Keen ability to find new solutions to challenging tasks while using both leadership and collaborative skills.
- Interest: Producing film, producing music, photography, basketball, tennis, baking and traveling.

EDUCATION

University of California, Davis   *September '10-Present*
    B.S. in **Management Economics** (Transferred from UCSC - Expected Graduation 2013)
University of California, Santa Cruz   *September '08-June '10*

POSSIBLE IMPROVEMENTS:

As I didn't change much from the previous resume, I could have improved in the same areas, such as design.

WHAT WORKED WELL:

- I replaced the volunteer radio experience with my new WBR experience.

- I changed the "Marketing internship" to just an intern, as I wasn't applying to a marketing position, so I wanted to keep it general.

- Honestly, the name of Warner Bros. Records got my foot in the door. As long as the experience is in the entertainment industry, it doesn't matter whether it's music or film.

- I added a line of interest, which is essentially my activities. I felt that Nickelodeon was more fun and wanted to know who I was and what I enjoyed doing.

DREAMWORKS ANIMATION STUDIO RESUME

When it came to the resume I sent to DreamWorks Animation Studio, it was basically the same.

ERIC BRAVO

(415) 555-5555 • youremail@gmail.com • 123 None. St. Hollywood, CA • www.eric-bravo.com

EXPERIENCE

Nickelodeon Animation Studios – Burbank, CA   *February '13-April '13*
Post Production/Vault Intern
- Archived digital and physical assets such as ProTools session and scripts for studio use and future preservation
- Documented and organized archived assets using FileMaker Pro
- Collaborated with co-interns to teach and inspire Jordan Middle School students about animation and the industry by creating classes and training materials
- Participated in business skills workshops to better understand the animation industry and departments
- Pitched a short as a writer in Nickelodeon's Animated Shorts Program

Warner Bros. Record – Burbank, CA   *September '12-December '12*
International Marketing Intern
- Facilitated publicity and promotional interviews between artists and foreign media
- Used Excel to maintain daily data sales to track the progress of every artist under Warner Bros. Records overseas
- Sent weekly management reports of the overseas sales to band managers
- Performed administrative tasks, such as data entry, answering phones, e-mailing, scanning and making copies

Colegio Chamberí – Madrid, Spain   *April '12-June '12*
Teacher's Assistant
- Assisted teachers with teaching English as a second language to first and second grade students
- Organized engaging group activities such as alphabet and color recognition games to promote English speaking

Sacramento Grant A Wish – Sacramento, California   *December '10-February '11*
Marketing Intern
- Developed media outlets and encouraged more traffic though Twitter, YouTube and Facebook
- Produced promotional videos to illustrate the mission statement and promote upcoming events to potential sponsors and volunteers
- Worked closely with managers and co-workers to ensure project deadlines were met

Delta Sigma Pi
Nu Rho Chapter – University of California, Davis   *September '10-Present*
Vice President of Alumni Relations (Winter/Spring 2011)
- Created a LinkedIn job postings group, sent bimonthly alumni email updates, and managed the Twitter account
- Organized and hosted an alumni panel open to the university student body
- Coordinated, maintained and oversaw the Alumni Mentorship Program
- Planned various alumni social events such as alumni picnic and alumni-collegiate basketball game

Pi Chi Chapter – University of California, Santa Cruz   *October '09-Present*
Founding Father
- Successfully established Delta Sigma Pi International Professional Fraternity at UC Santa Cruz
- Collaborated with a group of diverse individuals to organize and promote professional and community service events
- Worked closely with other members to raise money for the colony and to ensure the efficient use of funds
- Completed various long-term tasks to ensure Delta Sigma Pi's prosperity at the university by creating the chapter's by-laws, rules and regulations.
- Designed the colony's first T-Shirt to promote recruitment week to potential prospects

SKILLS/ACTIVITIES

- Computer: Mac/PC literate, proficient in MS Office Suite, Apple's Logic Pro 9, GarageBand, Final Cut Pro and Aperture and fundamental use of Final Draft and Adobe's Photoshop CS6, Dreamweaver CS6, and Affect Effects CS6
- Leadership: Student Union Assembly Representative (Spring '09); College 10 Senate Member (Jan '09-June'10)
- Work Style: Passionate, motivated, takes initiative, detail and goal oriented; keen ability to find new solutions to challenging tasks while using both leadership and collaborative skills
- Interests: Producing film, producing music, photography, tennis, karate, baking, background extra work and traveling

EDUCATION

University of California, Davis   *September '10-Present*
   Bachelors of Science degree in **Management Economics** (Expected Graduation 2013)
University of California, Santa Cruz   *September '08-June '10*

WHAT WORKED WELL:

- I put bullet points between each section of the contact information to make it easier to read.

- I took it out the pointless objective.

- I changed the heading and finally capitalized my name!

- I tried to make the design a bit more pleasing to the eye.

- I included my Nickelodeon Animation Studio experience and my study aboard internship experience.

- I improved on my bullet points for the Warner Bros. Records position.

- I added teacher's assistant, because I figured if DreamWorks is geared towards a younger audience, this might help in some way.

- I also improved on the fraternity bullet points.

I hope these resume improvements and mistakes will help you on your resume journey.

How To Write A Cover Letter

A cover letter accompanies your resume to give recruiters a detailed explanation of your work experience. Cover letters are personal and should be tailored to each specific company and position. Your goal in the cover letter is to explain how your experience makes you an ideal candidate for the position you're applying for. Although not all internships require cover letters, it's still best to send one regardless, as it can make your application stand out.

In the cover letter, you need to introduce yourself and state your intentions. It's also a chance to display how well you communicate in writing. You need to explain how your previous work experience will translate into this position, and how you can help the company grow if you are given the internship.

Here are a couple of things to bear in mind when crafting your cover letter.

DON'T COPY YOUR RESUME BULLET POINTS VERBATIM

Unlike the phrases in your resume, you need to write in full sentences in your cover letter, but don't just copy and paste your resume bullet points. You need to elaborate using complete sentences and add details. The cover letter should roughly be a less than a page long. You don't want to bombard the recruiter with a ton of information, but you also want to demonstrate that you are the right student for the internship. It should include an introduction, two paragraphs describing your experience, and a conclusion paragraph.

RESEARCH THE STUDIO BEFOREHAND

Because cover letters are so personal to each job you're applying for, you need to understand the studio's culture and environment so you can explain how you'd fit in. For example, if you're applying to Pixar's internship program, head over to their website and find the "Our Story" section in the "About" page.

Familiarize yourself with the company's history and explain how you and your skills would fit into their culture.

ALWAYS DOUBLE-CHECK YOUR LETTER

Once you have a solid cover letter, you can use it as a template to send to different studios, tailored to the position of course. However, you must remember to change the studio's name! This seems like a no brainer, but when you're applying to many studios and have been sending a lot of cover letters, things get repetitive and you get a bit lazy. I am guilty of this too! So, here's a cautionary tale.

When I applied to DreamWorks, I was collecting my recent resume and my cover letter to reuse. I wrote an email and attached my cover letter and resume along with it. I had just applied to Pixar moments before and had that resume and cover letter on my desktop. After I sent my application to Pixar, I wanted to quickly finish sending all of my applications. I attached the Pixar resume and cover letter to the DreamWorks email…and I hit send. I double-checked my sent inbox just to make sure it went through, and clicked the attachments to see whether they were correct. I opened up the cover letter and saw that it was addressed to Pixar Animation Studio instead of DreamWorks! I thought I had messed up my chances for good. The lesson of the story is always double-check before you submit.

Luckily for me, the story didn't end there. I actually got a call back from the DreamWorks recruiter to set up an interview. I was shocked! I confessed my mistake to the recruiter and asked whether she could update my cover letter with the correct studio name before she sent it to the interviewers. She said, "Sure! That's no problem at all."

Fast forward to my in-person DreamWorks interview with three different departments. I walked into the first interview, and the first thing I saw was my cover letter in the interviewer's hand with "Pixar Animation Studios" highlighted. Not a first great impression! I couldn't even explain my terrible mistake, except that I hadn't double-checked my work, which wasn't a quality they look for. Much to my surprise, I ended up with an internship on the movie *Penguins of Madagascar*. I'm as clueless as you probably are right now, just how I got an internship at DreamWorks with my cover letter mistakenly addressed to Pixar! I'm assuming they were impressed with my prior internships and knew it was an honest mistake. I'm just happy that a scary situation turned into a funny story. Don't take the risk!

If you use Gmail, there is an option to unsend an email within a 30-second window. This has come in handy for me many times! Go to settings and the "General" tab should be displayed. If not, find it and click on it. Under "Undo Send" check the box next to "Enable Undo Send" to turn on this feature. Underneath that, you'll find "Send cancellation period" with a drop-down arrow list. Your options are 5, 10, 20, or 30 seconds. I have mine set for 30 seconds. I always double-check my email prior to hitting the send button, but I use this function so I can triple-check my e-mail as it is sending. In case you forgot to add or attach something, you can always undo the email before it reaches the person's inbox.

CRAFTING YOUR COVER LETTER

This is my current cover letter, which I'll go through in order.

ERIC BRAVO

Cover Letter

Dear Walt Disney Animation Studio:

As my enclosed resume indicates, I have a degree in Managerial Economics from the University of California, Davis and have been involved in the entertainment industry for a couple of years. I created a cartoon short with Nickelodeon Animation Studios and worked closely with the directors, artist, and producers. As an intern at Nickelodeon, I helped manage the art archives and used FileMaker Pro to keep various assets organized and up to date.

In addition, I have also interned with DreamWorks Animation Studios in the Production Department where I updated and maintained various materials, such as dialogue scripts and story layouts, to ensure all were up to date for meetings and recordings. I improved on my ability to prioritize and multi-task and provided administrative support to multiple departments including scheduling, data entry, event planning, and organizing digital artwork through meta-data entry.

During my time with Google's Self-Driving Car Project, I managed various projects simultaneously including a multi-month build project with high priority data requests. I planned and executed operations in an efficient and timely fashion and communicated to keep the team on track to meet our dynamic deadlines. Working on a new technology involved working in a highly secure environment as well as frequent encounters and resolution of unexpected issues.

I have also interned at Warner Bros. Records in the International Marketing Department. In this fast-paced environment, I was in charge of gathering sales data of all of Warner Bros. Records' artist from the overseas market and putting them into excel documents to track the sales of the week, both physical and digital sales. I assisted the VP of International Marketing with daily office needs such as emailing industry professionals, preparing their materials for weekly meetings, and handling phones. I was responsible for attending marketing meetings and took notes for current and upcoming projects. I facilitated the logistics of company events, created weekly management reports, and handled special projects as requested.

Overall, I believe I can contribute to the team by being detail-oriented, having effective time management and follow-up skills, and having the ability to produce accurate work in a timely fashion. I am confident that my ability to work within a team environment and my firm desire to take initiative and offer high quality work will prove beneficial at Walt Disney Animation. Thank you for your time and I look forward to hearing back soon.

Sincerely,

Eric Bravo

OVERALL DESIGN:

As you can tell, it's formatted with a similar design to my current resume. You should keep both of these documents consistent as it shows you are detail-oriented and organized.

HEADER:

In the header, I include my name in bold, and underneath I include the words "Cover Letter." You can put the position you are applying instead of "Cover Letter." This is a personal choice.

ADDRESSED TO:

You need to address the cover letter to the studio you are applying to. In this example, it is addressed to Walt Disney Animation Studio. I bolded their name to make it stand out from the body of the cover letter and increased the size subtly. You can also address it, "Dear Walt Disney Recruiting:" if you want another option.

I also used to include the company's address in the cover letter. It is a more traditional way of formatting your cover letter. Now, I don't think it's necessary as we are moving to a more digital workplace and aren't physically sending the cover letter to the company.

OPENING PARAGRAPH:

The opening paragraph should be two or three sentences stating your education, what position you are applying for, and why you want the position. Also explain why you are a good fit for it. In my more recent cover letters, I jump straight into my experience because I want to cover a lot. In my previous cover letter to Nickelodeon (found later in this chapter), you'll see how I listed out everything: the position I was applying to, what Nickelodeon's culture was like, and how I fit in.

MIDDLE PARAGRAPHS:

The middle paragraphs should summarize your resume highlights. Explain in more detail how your experience aligns to what the company is looking for in an intern. You also want to explain what you can offer to the studio.

CLOSING PARAGRAPH:

The closing paragraph should be two or three sentences summarizing how you might be a good fit. You want to explain how you can contribute, but also how you can learn from this position. The last sentence should thank them for their time. Always end the letter with "Sincerely" and then your name.

MY PAST COVER LETTERS

Now you can see my previous cover letters, again in chronological order, so you can see the progression. As with the resumes, I'll review them to see what worked well and what didn't. This is also something you should do from time to time with your cover letter.

WARNER BROS. RECORDS COVER LETTER

This is the original cover letter that got me the International Marketing Internship at Warner Bros. Records.

Eric Bravo
123 None St.
Hollywood, CA 91503
(415) 555-5555
youremail@gmail.com

Warner Bros. Records
Los Angeles, CA

To Whom It May Concern:

I am currently in my fourth year of a BS Managerial Economics Degree at the University of California, Davis. It is my deepest intent to apply for your Fall Internship Position as promoted online on your website. It has became evident to me that Warner Bros. Records strives to foster not only excellent professional services within the music entertainment industry, but also an environment where its employees and clients can learn, grow, and excel. I believe that my commitment to excellence, willingness to learn, and passion and discipline toward the work performed are consistent with Warner Bros. Records' values and aims.

Along with this letter, I have enclosed my resume, which outlines some of my qualifications. I have become involved in a number of rich extracurricular activities that will allow me to contribute to your organization and its work. These activities include holding various leadership positions within Delta Sigma Pi, a professional business Fraternity which enhances personal and team driven success through finance, community service, social, and professional events and workshops. Overall, I am confident that my ability to work within a team environment and my resolute desire to take initiative and offer high quality work will prove beneficial at Warner Bros. Records.

I am excited to learn more about the music entertainment industry and gain more insight into some of the activities that Warner Bros. Records conducts. I believe my motivation, assertiveness, organization and ability to find solutions to challenging tasks make me an ideal intern for your program. Thank you for your time and consideration.

Sincerely,

Eric Bravo

POSSIBLE IMPROVEMENTS:

- It's simple—just a Word document. I don't know how I got 3 out of 4 interviews for that!

- The proportions are off, as it seems a bit top heavy with all of the information squeezed at the top and a ton of space at the bottom.

- My name looks horrible, and it's a very basic header.

- I included all the necessary information, but it feels a bit squished.

- I made a mistake with the location of Warner Bros. Records. It is in Burbank specifically, not in Los Angeles, which isn't a huge deal, but could be better.

- Although there's nothing wrong with "To Whom It May Concern," it's better to address the company, for example: "Dear Warner Bros. Records."

- I should have mentioned something about volunteering at the radio station.

WHAT WORKED WELL:

- I explained that I believed in WBR's culture, which showed that I cared and had researched the company.

- I ended the paragraph with how my skills and personality aligned with their culture, which is great.

NICKELODEON ANIMATION STUDIO COVER LETTER

Here is the original cover letter that got me the Vault Intern role at Nickelodeon Animation Studio.

Eric Bravo

Phone: (415) 555-5555   *Email:* youremail@gmail.com

Address: 123 None St. Hollywood, CA

Nickelodeon Animation Studios:
231 W Olive Ave
Burbank, CA 91502

Dear Nickelodeon Animation Studios:

I am currently enrolled at the University of California, Davis in pursuit of a B.S. Managerial Economics Degree. It is my deepest intent to apply for your Internship Position. It has became evident to me that Nickelodeon Animation Studios strives to foster not only creativity and enjoyment within the entertainment industry, but also an environment where its employees can learn, grow, and excel. I believe that my commitment to excellence, willingness to learn, creativity, and passion and discipline toward the work performed are consistent with Nickelodeon Animation Studios' values and aims.

Along with this letter, I have enclosed my resume, which outlines some of my qualifications. I have become involved in a number of rich extracurricular activities that will allow me to contribute to your organization and its work. These activities include holding various leadership positions within Delta Sigma Pi, a professional business Fraternity which enhances personal and team driven success through finance, community service, social, and professional events and workshops.

I am currently an intern at Warner Bros. Records in the International Marketing Department where I am learning how to communicate with both company executives and external VIPs such as band managers while also developing my office responsibilities including scheduling, e-mailing, scanning, and handling phone calls. I am expected to follow complex and precise directions in order to keep the company's high profile music clientele satisfied. Overall, I am confident that my ability to work within a team environment and my resolute desire to take initiative and offer high quality work will prove beneficial at Nickelodeon Animation Studios.

I am excited to learn more about the entertainment industry and gain more insight into some of the activities that Nickelodeon Animation Studios conducts. I believe my motivation, assertiveness, organization and ability to find solutions to challenging tasks make me an ideal intern for your program. Thank you for your time and consideration.

Sincerely,

Eric Bravo

WHAT WORKED WELL:

This is a much better-looking cover letter, and is more professional than my WBR one. You can just feel this cover letter oozing professionalism.

- I improved on the header and organized it a bit more.

- I added another paragraph explaining my duties at Warner Bros. Records. This makes the cover letter much fuller.

- I came to my senses and got rid of the many, many, many spaces between "Sincerely" and my name.

POSSIBLE IMPROVEMENTS:

- The first "(" in the phone number is in bold. This was a mistake that I made when sending in the cover letter. Remember, don't be lazy and always double-check your work! These small details matter. I just got lucky.

DREAMWORKS ANIMATION STUDIO COVER LETTER

This is the original cover letter that got me the Production Intern role at DreamWorks Animation.

ERIC BRAVO

(415) 555-5555 • youremail@gmail.com • 123 None St. Hollywood, CA 95103 • www.eric-bravo.com

Dreamworks Animation Studios
1400 - A Seaport Boulevard
Redwood City, CA 94063

Dear Dreamworks Animation Studios:

I am currently enrolled at the University of California, Davis in pursuit of a B.S. Managerial Economics Degree. It is my deepest intent to apply for your Production Intern position. It is evident to me that Dreamworks Animation Studios strives to foster not only creativity and enjoyment within the entertainment industry, but also an environment where its employees can learn, grow, and excel. I believe that my commitment to excellence, willingness to learn, creativity, and passion are consistent with Dreamworks Animation Studios' values and aims.

Along with this letter, I have enclosed my resume, which outlines some of my qualifications. I have become involved in a number of rich extracurricular activities that will allow me to contribute to your organization and its work. These activities include holding various leadership positions within Delta Sigma Pi, a professional business Fraternity which enhances personal and team driven success through finance, community service, social, and professional events and workshops.

I recently interned at Nickelodeon Animation Studios in the Post Production/Vault Department where I learned a great deal about the animation industry and had the opportunity to pitch a short as a writer to Mary Harington and Julian James that reached the high executive level review. Last fall I interned at Warner Bros. Records in the International Marketing Department where I learned how to communicate with both company executives and external VIPs such as band managers. I followed complex and precise directions in order to keep the company's high profile music clientele satisfied and was able to develop my office skills by supporting the administrative needs of the department. I am confident that my ability to work within a team environment and my resolute desire to take initiative and offer high quality work will prove beneficial at Pixar Animation Studios.

I am excited to learn more about the entertainment industry and gain more insight into some of the activities that Dreamworks Animation Studios conducts. I believe my motivation, assertiveness, organization and ability to find solutions to challenging tasks make me an ideal intern for this position. Thank you for your time and consideration.

Sincerely,

Eric Bravo

- It's looking a bit fuller, which is perfect.

- I capitalized my name and made the contact information a bit easier to read. It's the same header as my resume, so feels consistent.

- I added an extra sentence about my Nickelodeon internship.

POSSIBLE IMPROVEMENTS:

- As you can clearly see in the last sentence of paragraph 3, here is the mistake: "…my resolute desire to take initiative and offer high quality work will prove beneficial at Pixar Animation Studios." H-O-L-Y…C-R-A-P. I had already sent my cover letter and resume to about two other positions at DreamWorks before I finally caught this!

- As you can see, I reviewed my cover letter and improved it over time. Despite making a huge mistake in calling the studio by the wrong name, my cover letter somehow still earned me an internship. If we can learn something from this, a mistake can be overlooked by a solid, well-crafted cover letter. So, you need to ensure you make yours great! However, learn from my mistake and always double-check your cover letter before you send it, especially when you're using a template cover letter.

Resume & Cover Letter Templates

You can download my resume and cover letter templates from my website: http://www.eric-bravo.com/resume-download. It is password protected. Be sure to include the word "internship" to access the download page.

Use my current resume and cover letter as seen in this book as inspiration. I've gotten a lot of great feedback from many recruiters that it looks clean, professional, and creatively detailed. Play around with the template, add a picture to the top left page, change the color of the side bar, try to customize it to your liking.

In the past, I've also found great templates from Pages (Mac's version of Word). I just go to their templates section when making a new document. They have pretty good templates. Google Docs also has a bunch of resume templates and so does Microsoft Word.

If you want to go professional with a slick design, check out Creative Market (www.creativemarket.com). Under their templates section, find "Resumes" and click on it. Here you'll find a bunch of beautifully designed resume temples. Some also include cover letters as well. You have to pay for these, but if they make your resume pop and it looks clean and professional, they're worth it.

If you're on a budget and you know how to use Photoshop or InDesign, you can always be inspired by a design and make it your own.

Q & A With Paula Gallagher

- Senior Production Assistant at Industrial Light & Magic

- Production Coordinator at Industrial Light & Magic

- Production Assistant at Industrial Light & Magic

- Facilities Assistant at DreamWorks

- Artistic Development Intern at DreamWorks

- Brand Ambassador for Nespresso

- Production Intern at Campos Creative Works

Paula had her eyes set on an animation internship early on and she eventually got her start as an Artistic Development Intern at DreamWorks Animation. After graduating from San Francisco State University, she landed a job as a Facilities Assistant at DreamWorks. Since the closure of the DreamWorks PDI office in Redwood City, Paula transitioned to a Production Assistant at Industrial Light and Magic.

Update: Since this interview, Paula switched companies to Industrial Light & Magic (ILM) and has worked on the new Star Wars movies where she animated two shots in *Rogue One: A Star Wars Story*. She is currently a Senior Production Assistant at ILM.

Q: WHAT COLLEGE DID YOU ATTEND AND WHAT WAS YOUR MAJOR? DO YOU THINK THIS HELPED WITH YOUR PURSUIT IN THE ENTERTAINMENT INDUSTRY?

I attended San Francisco State University. I majored in Creative Writing and minored in Animation. I think it certainly helped my pursuit in the film industry. I actually knew very little about the film industry before I started the Animation Emphasis at SFSU (an intensive 2-year program with a very small number of students).

Q: WHEN DID YOU KNOW YOU WANTED TO BE IN THE ENTERTAINMENT/ANIMATION INDUSTRY AND WHAT EVENTS LED YOU TO CHOOSE IT?

I've always been very interested in Animation and I loved animated films, but I honestly knew very little about how they were made. I applied to the Animation Emphasis at SFSU and admitted in my interview that I had never animated before, but that I was a fast learner and very hard working. I was surprised when I got into the program, but very eager to learn. I quickly fell in love with animation, particularly when I began to learn character acting animation.

Q: DID ANYONE/ANYTHING INSPIRE YOU TO FOLLOW YOUR PASSION FOR ENTERTAINMENT?

My best friend Nicole Casado has supported everything creative that I've ever done. From when I was a kid writing short stories to when I began learning animation, she has always been so supportive and excited to see my work. Honestly, it's hard to pursue something creative if there isn't someone in your life encouraging you, so I am very grateful for her.

Also, my boss while I was an intern, Victor Fuste, was inspirational. I knew very little about character animation when I came to DreamWorks, and had done almost no animation in 3D. He gave me one-on-one animation classes, and taught me how to do walk cycles and character acting. I am very grateful for that.

Q: YOU STARTED OFF AS A PRODUCTION INTERN AT CAMPOS CREATIVE WORKS IN SANTA MONICA, CA. HOW DID THAT HELP GET YOU TO WHERE YOU ARE NOW?

Creative works is an event production company that puts on large scale corporate events. The summer that I interned with them, I was helping out with the Toyota Lifetime Fitness Event. Although I wasn't working in film, the internship definitely taught me how to function in a fast-paced production environment, and it was very helpful.

Q: FROM THERE, YOU BECAME A BRAND AMBASSADOR FOR NESPRESSO. WHAT DID THAT ENTAIL?

I worked in that job part time while I was in my last two years of college. I would go to different locations that sold Nespresso Products and make samples, and sometimes train employees on how to work the machines. It's a job that I would definitely recommend to students. I did it while interning at DreamWorks, and they were quite flexible with my schedule.

Q: HOW DID YOU LAND THE ARTISTIC DEVELOPMENT INTERNSHIP AT DREAMWORKS ANIMATION? WHAT DID YOU DO THERE?

I applied with my resume, cover letter, and link to my online portfolio. After about a week, I got a call inviting me for an interview. As an Artistic Development Intern, it was my job to make posters and slides for in-house events using Photoshop. In the Training department, they offered all kinds of classes for employees, such as drawing, design, and their animation software PREMO. The posters and slides promoted these events and classes.

Q: WHAT WAS THE APPLICATION AND INTERVIEW PROCESS LIKE?

It was very straightforward. I went in for an interview and was offered the internship within the next couple of days. The recruiters were very friendly and explained that the internship was a great way to learn about the company.

Q: WHAT DO YOU THINK SET YOUR APPLICATION/INTERVIEW APART FROM OTHERS?

I think I wrote a pretty strong cover letter, and the interview went very well, so I'm sure that helped. My boss was also interested in the fact that I was studying both animation and creative writing. It stood out to him on my resume.

Q: WHAT WAS THE INTERNSHIP EXPERIENCE LIKE OVERALL?

The internship was great. I learned so much, and it was good to meet so many talented people. My boss set up meetings for the interns to speak to artists and production staff. It was very interesting to learn about all the different departments in the company, and it really made me think about what direction I wanted to take my career in within the film industry.

Q: WHAT WAS THE BEST PART ABOUT BEING A DREAMWORKS INTERN?

For me, it was access to their proprietary animation software PREMO. I was set up with a shot and character rig. I was also allowed to take the work I did using their rigs and put it on my reel.

Q: ANY ADVICE TO STUDENTS APPLYING TO THE DREAMWORKS INTERNSHIP PROGRAM?

Keep checking the website and apply as soon as the internship is posted. This shows that you're interested, and guarantees that someone will see it. Make sure your resume has your schooling at the top, because the first rule of being an intern is that you must be a student. Make your resume neat and easy to read, and write a short, concise cover letter.

Q: ANY ADVICE TO STUDENTS WHO JUST GOT ACCEPTED INTO THE INTERNSHIP PROGRAM THAT YOU WISH YOU HAD KNOWN?

Talk to as many people as you can, and don't be afraid to ask questions. I was very shy when I began as an intern. It wasn't until I got a full-time job that I began opening up and asking other employees questions about their jobs, and how they got where they are today. Making connections is very important, so if you are quiet like me, it's good to step outside your comfort zone.

Q: HOW LONG CAN YOU INTERN AT DREAMWORKS?

I believe you can intern for as many semesters as you want, provided you are a student and that they want you to continue.

Q: AFTER YOUR INTERNSHIP AS AN ARTISTIC DEVELOPMENT INTERN, YOU BECAME A FACILITIES ASSISTANT AT PDI/DREAMWORKS. HOW DID YOU TRANSITION FROM BEING AN INTERN TO BECOMING A FULL-TIME EMPLOYEE?

At DreamWorks, Facilities is well-known as a good way to get your foot in the door. I became interested in getting a job in Facilities as my graduation was approaching, and it seemed like a good way to continue with the company and eventually move into a production or an artistic role. There are always three Facilities Assistants at one time, and one of them who was a friend of mine had just been promoted. She encouraged me to meet with her boss, and learn more about the job. I was called in the following week for an interview, and was offered a job the week after that.

Some of the tasks include: delivering mail, sending out interoffice mail, coordinating and managing large scale events, and connecting phones for new employees. In general, every day in facilities can be different from the last. It's a very fast-paced job, but it really helped me learn how to think on my feet and multitask.

Now that I have been here a year, and this location for DreamWorks is unfortunately closing before I ever got to advance, I've also been asked to take over some Production Assistant tasks. I often take notes for meetings, and sometimes "drive," by pulling up artists' work for them.

Q: WHAT WAS THE APPLICATION AND INTERVIEW PROCESS LIKE?

It was very straightforward. I interviewed with my two supervisors. They explained that the job is quite intensive, but that it's a great way to get your foot in the door and make connections.

Q: WHAT DO YOU THINK SET YOUR APPLICATION/INTERVIEW APART FROM OTHERS?

The fact that I was a former intern definitely helped, because I had a good idea of what the job was. I was also lucky to have a friend who had just been promoted from facilities and recommended me.

Q: HAVING WORKED AT THE PDI/DREAMWORKS OFFICE FOR SEVERAL YEARS, HOW DO YOU FEEL ABOUT IT SHUTTING DOWN?

It's very sad that PDI/DreamWorks will be shutting down. I honestly thought I would be at PDI for a very long time. The people here are so talented and inspiring, and I'm very sad that I won't be working with them anymore.

Either way, I have made some wonderful friends, and am so glad that I got the chance to work here.

Q: WHERE DO YOU HOPE TO BE IN 5 YEARS?

I hope to be an animator. Ideally, I would love to be working in feature films, but I would be happy to work in games as well.

Q: WHAT IS YOUR DREAM PROJECT?

I'd love to pitch an idea for an animated film to DreamWorks. It would be amazing to work on something with a story that I developed.

Q: WHAT HAS BEEN YOUR PROUDEST MOMENT SO FAR?

Finishing my first character acting shot in PREMO. Before interning at DreamWorks, I had only animated in 2D, and really wanted to learn 3D character animation, but I wasn't sure whether I was good enough. As of right now, I still don't think I'm good enough, but I do think that I'm improving, which gives me hope that someday I can turn it into a career.

Q: WHAT'S THE BEST ADVICE YOU CAN GIVE YOUR PAST SELF, KNOWING WHAT YOU KNOW NOW?

I would probably tell my past self to decide exactly what area I wanted to specialize in, and work on only that. When I began animation in school, I wasn't sure whether I wanted to do storyboarding, layout, or animation. I wish that I had figured out what I wanted to do a little bit sooner.

Q: FAVORITE FILM AND/OR TV SHOW?

How to Train Your Dragon. After seeing that film, I began to seriously consider a career in animation. A close second is *Treasure Planet*, as I think that film is visually stunning.

Q: ANY WORK YOU WOULD LIKE TO SHARE?

My animation demo reel: https://vimeo.com/119262180

CHAPTER 3

Applying For Internships

The Animation Studios

Most students are only familiar with the major animation studios and don't think of applying to smaller ones, but doing so can increase your chances of getting into the animation industry. Here, I have complied a list of various animation studios for you. I've included studios from the United States, as well as international, major, and smaller studios. This list should give you many internships to apply to. Research the studios, find out what work they have done, and apply to the studios that really interest you.

MAJOR STUDIOS

California

- Pixar Animation Studios - Emeryville, CA
- Lucasfilm Animation - San Francisco, CA
- Industrial Light & Magic - San Francisco, CA
- Walt Disney Animation Studios - Burbank, CA
- Nickelodeon Animation Studios - Burbank, CA
- Cartoon Network Studios - Burbank, CA
- Adult Swim - Burbank, CA
- Warner Bros. Animation - Burbank, CA
- Disney Television Animation - Glendale, CA
- DisneyToon Studios - Glendale, CA
- DreamWorks Animation Studios - Glendale, CA
- Sony Pictures Animation - Culver City, CA

- 20th Century Fox Animation - Los Angeles, CA

New York

- Marvel Studios - New York, NY

Oregon

- LAIKA - Hillsboro, OR

Connecticut

- Blue Sky Studio - Greenwich, Connecticut

Georgia

Adult Swim - Atlanta, GA

SMALLER STUDIOS

- Atomic Fiction - Oakland, CA
- Acme Filmworks - Los Angeles, CA
- Bento Box Entertainment - North Hollywood, CA
- Frederator Studios - New York, NY/Burbank, CA
- Titmouse - Los Angeles, CA
- Fuzzy Door Productions - Los Angeles, CA
- Method Studios - Los Angeles, CA
- Rhythm & Hues Studios - Los Angeles, CA
- Frame Machine - Santa Monica, CA
- Luma Pictures - Santa Monica, CA
- South Park Studios - Culver City, CA
- Zoic Studios - Culver City, CA
- Rough Draft Studios - Glendale CA

- Encore Hollywood - Hollywood, CA
- Digital Domain - Playa Vista, California

GAMING STUDIOS

- Blizzard Entertainment - Multiple Locations
- Electronic Arts - Multiple Locations

INTERNATIONAL STUDIOS

Asia

- Studio Ghibli - Koganei, Tokyo, Japan
- Nippon Animation – Tokyo, Japan
- Sunrise - Suginami, Tokyo, Japan
- Studio 4°C - Tokyo, Japan
- Madhouse - Tokyo, Japan
- Toei Animation – Tokyo, Japan

Europe

- Framestone - London, England
- Double Negative - Fitzrovia, London, England
- Elstree Studio, London, England

New Zealand

- Weta Digital - Wellington, NZ

Australia

- Rubber House - Melbourne

Canada

- Atomic Fiction - Montreal, Quebec, Canada

- Sony Pictures Imageworks - Vancouver, Canada

Where To Find Available Internships

There are multiple ways to find available animation internships. In this chapter, I'll be going over some of the methods for finding them. Be cautious when looking for an internship as most programs have deadlines and their internship applications are only available prior to the start of their programs (Fall, Spring, Summer).

COMPANY'S CAREER PAGE

Use the list from the previous section to find the studio's career page via their website and apply online. You can also ask whether you can volunteer at the smaller studios. Of course, this would be on your own time and dollar, but it's still a great way to build connections.

LINKEDIN

You can set alarms on LinkedIn to alert you when there are animation internships available. You'll be notified via the LinkedIn app or email. You can also reach out to university/college recruiters via LinkedIn. This is a great way to build connections and get your name out there. You can also reach out to employees who were once interns, as they might know about upcoming internships. This way, you can build a connection and who knows, they might keep you in mind if something pops up. Here is a template email you can send to them. In the email, remember to respect their time.

Dear (insert name),

I have a huge interest in building a career in animation. While searching on LinkedIn for potential internship opportunities at (insert studio name here), your name popped up.

I wanted to ask you more about working in animation and (insert company name). (Insert company name) has been a place I have always wanted to work because... (insert your personal thoughts here).

If you aren't too busy, would it be possible to meet for coffee or schedule a phone call?

I hope you are doing well. Have an amazing week!

Sincerely,

Your Name

GLASSDOOR

Glassdoor is another great resource to find available internships. It's an employment website that offers job opportunities, salary information, and interview questions from candidates who applied to that specific position. Not only that, but the website also includes information on the company's culture from past interns and employees.

YOUTUBE CREATORS

Another method is going to the animation section on YouTube and reaching out to creators. Ask whether you can help them out in anyway. With this route, you can learn remotely on your own time.

The Best Time To Apply

Most students apply for internships during the summer months, which makes these programs very competitive, especially for the highly sought after studios. If you want to better your chances, apply during the **off-seasons** (the Fall/Spring semester) instead, and take some classes at your university during the summer. This way, you can still be on track for your graduation date while also building your work experience.

I know what you might be thinking—"Hey I don't want to miss taking classes with friends!" or "Off-season internships aren't paid, but summer is!" or just "Wait, what? I thought they only had summer internships." Hold on just a minute. Before you claim your summer back, consider this.

All of my internships were either during the Fall or Spring semester. I applied to Warner Bros. Records for the Summer program and didn't hear back from them. I then re-applied for the Fall program without changing a single thing on my resume and received *three* interviews—all in various departments.

The reason for this is because Summer is filled with internship applicants. So, I recommend applying during the off-season such as Fall or Spring, as you're more likely to secure an internship then. During summer, take summer school instead. Sure, you'll miss hanging out with your friends during the regular school year, but there are plenty of people there during summer too, and in my personal opinion, you actually grow closer in summer school.

If you really want an internship, you have to make some sacrifices. With that said, however, still apply every chance you get, including to the Summer internships. It's free, so why not? There's always a possibility.

Preparing Your Online Application

Okay, the time has finally arrived! You planned ahead and spent time building your work experience. You wrote the perfect resume and cover letter, and now you're ready to start your application. But before you get started, let's go over how to prepare for your online application.

DON'T APPLY TO EVERY SINGLE ROLE

Recruiters can see how many positions you have applied for, and it doesn't look good if you apply to every single internship available. I recommend picking your top three choices and only apply to those.

WHEN YOU APPLY

Now you know which internships you're applying for, it's time to actually apply. When you do, bear in mind the following tips:

1.Proofread your resume and check it yourself, then have two other people proofread it as well. The more eyes, the better.

2.If you don't know anyone who can do this, there are websites such as Fiverr where you can hire someone, but remember that you get what you pay for, so if you want a great edit, you'll have to pay a bit more than $5.00!

3.Export your resume and cover letter into a PDF document format. This makes it look clean and professional.

4.Proofread it again.

5.Each studio has a different application process, so make sure you read it carefully before you hit the submit button.

DON'T FORGET THE DEADLINES

Be mindful when you apply, as there are deadlines for internship applications. Mark your calendars with the deadlines so you don't miss them!

Q & A With Lily Zaldivar

- Video Producer at Wish

- Production Coordinator at IGN Entertainment

- VFX Production Coordinator at Industrial Light & Magic

- VFX 2D Coordinator on *Kubo and the Two Strings* at LAIKA

- VFX Production Assistant at LAIKA

- Production Assistant at Atomic Film

- Receptionist for WB Games and Flixter at Warner Bros. Entertainment

- Videography Intern at DreamWorks

During Lily's time at San Francisco State University, she got her internship start as a Videography Intern at DreamWorks Animation in the old PDI/DreamWorks office. Upon graduation, she landed a job at Warner Bros. Entertainment. After Lily's stint at Warner Bros., she headed up north to LAIKA and became heavily involved in the Production department starting off as an intern and working her way up to a VFX 2D Coordinator.

Update: Since this interview, Lily worked as a Production Coordinator at Industrial Light & Magic on the new Star Wars movies and is currently working as a Video Producer at Wish.

Q: WHAT COLLEGE DID YOU ATTEND AND WHAT WAS YOUR MAJOR? DO YOU THINK THIS HELPED WITH YOUR PURSUIT IN THE ENTERTAINMENT INDUSTRY?

I attended San Francisco State University and my major was Cinema with an emphasis on animation. To be honest, my decision to work in the film industry started in high school thanks to my teachers Jude Lucas and Doug Ryneson. They really taught me how to be diligent with my work and how amazing being a part of a film crew or theater company could be.

Q: WHEN DID YOU KNOW YOU WANTED TO BE IN THE ENTERTAINMENT/ANIMATION INDUSTRY AND WHAT EVENTS LED YOU TO CHOOSE IT?

My pursuit in animation started in college. I was afraid that to be in animation, you must be able to draw, and I don't have much confidence in my drawing skills. But I got accepted and my pursuit of an animation career began.

Q: DID ANYONE/ANYTHING INSPIRE YOU TO FOLLOW YOUR PASSION FOR ENTERTAINMENT/ANIMATION?

My teachers and parents inspired me to pursue my dreams. My parents never told me I couldn't do anything. They would always tell me to do my best. When I left for college, I reminded myself to do my best and pursue what I want to do.

Q: AS A PRODUCTION ASSISTANT, WHAT DO YOUR DAILY TASKS CONSIST OF?

My daily tasks include: aiding my coordinators with any tasks they need, compiling notes during VFX Dailies, providing working lunch and working dinner. I help the executive assistant with morale boosters (such as beer and ice cream). I also create submission documents and shot magnets for certain movies.

Q: WAS PRODUCTION SOMETHING YOU ALWAYS WANTED TO PURSUE, OR DID YOU EVENTUALLY WANT TO SWITCH PATHS?

Initially, I wanted to do Editorial. I learned how to edit on Final Cut 7 as a freshman in high school and I really wanted to be an editor as I grew up. I also wanted to be an animator, but the chance to learn never came up. I also wanted to be an actress, but I thought Production would be a good fit for myself. I chose Production because it has all of the qualities I like. I work with artists to figure out a schedule that will benefit both the artist and the production team, I handle conversations with clients or with directors, and I am the support for the team.

Q: HOW WOULD YOU DESCRIBE THE CULTURE AT ATOMIC FICTION?

The culture is very relaxed, but also stressful. You never know when a shot is going to be pushed back from client. The most important aspect about the job is that the work we do isn't for in-house. It's for someone else's movie, so we have to work on someone else's vision for the film. But when a film is done or when every shot is final, it's a giant weight off your shoulders until we start the next film.

Q: HOW DID YOU SCORE THE VIDEOGRAPHY INTERNSHIP AT PDI/DREAMWORKS ANIMATION?

I just applied—that's about it really! I didn't know anyone at DreamWorks, and applying was a giant Hail Mary. I didn't really know what was going to happen, but Victor Fuste (my supervisor) and I hit it off during the interview process. Little did he know that I would be his worst nightmare, haha!

Q: WHAT DID YOU DO AS A VIDEOGRAPHY INTERN?

I edited classes that were recorded earlier in the day or month by Jonathan, the videographer at PDI. I also did other tasks such as photocopy handouts, print out new hire packs, and set up rooms for art shows. It was pretty fun!

Q: WHAT WAS YOUR COOLEST MOMENT?

The coolest moment will always be the Peabody and Sherman wrap party. I had never been to a wrap party before and it was off the hook! That and receiving gifts every now and then from DreamWorks was cool too!

Q: ANY ADVICE TO STUDENTS APPLYING TO DREAMWORKS INTERNSHIP POSITIONS?

You don't have to know someone to get an internship there. It helps, but it's important that in your resume, you show the skills that you've learned throughout college. If you have work experience at a retail or food place, explain the skill and how it applies to the internship you're trying to get. Overall, just convey your passion for the job you have or the classes you take. Having passion goes a long way.

Q: ANY ADVICE TO STUDENTS WHO JUST GOT ACCEPTED INTO THE INTERNSHIP THAT YOU WISH YOU HAD KNOWN?

It's not always fun and glamorous. Getting an internship means working hard to prove why you earned it. I've seen interns get internships at DreamWorks and then half way through the semester, they never show up to work. You're there for a reason. Prove why you're there.

Q: WHAT'S THE BEST PART ABOUT BEING A DREAMWORKS INTERN?

Making connections and making friends. A year after my internship, I'm working with people who I briefly met at DreamWorks. Everyone is so nice to each other and everyone at PDI wants you to succeed and fulfill your dreams.

Q: WHAT WAS THE INTERNSHIP EXPERIENCE LIKE OVERALL?

It was good. I learned a lot about DreamWorks as a business, and a lot about what I want to do in the Animation industry. If I hadn't been an intern there, I wouldn't have known that I would rather be a PA than an editorial assistant.

Q: HOW DO YOU FEEL ABOUT PDI/DREAMWORKS ANIMATION SHUTTING DOWN?

Oh man. That's a tough subject to talk about. When I found out, I was crushed. Not because of my chances of coming back, but because no one at PDI deserved to be let go. There are good people at PDI who have put their heart and soul into the characters or environments in DreamWorks films, and to see them all let go was heartbreaking.

Q: LIVING AND WORKING IN SAN FRANCISCO, DO YOU THINK IT IS POSSIBLE TO HAVE A SUCCESSFUL CAREER IN ENTERTAINMENT? OR IS IT NECESSARY TO MOVE TO HOLLYWOOD/LA, THE ENTERTAINMENT CAPITAL?

It depends on what you want to do to be honest. Each location has a different type of film industry. San Francisco has more VFX houses and independent film/documentary film houses, while LA has more major studios that people know, such as Warner Bros. and Disney. The way I think of it is—if you're willing to give San Francisco companies a try, then you may find companies who are like family and who are willing to teach you. In LA, companies like Disney and Warner want you to already know what you're doing, where you're going in your life, and what it takes to get the job done. No messing around and no f*** ups are allowed, because one giant mistake and you're replaced with the next person who applies. Everyone is replaceable in LA.

It was a learning experience, but I'm grateful for that job because it put me on the right path to my career. Although I wasn't doing what I wanted, I learned during the first months what I liked and didn't like in a job. I learned to become organized and help out as much as I could. I don't think any other job would have taught me that.

It was amazing! They really should start doing those again. I have no words to describe how great it was to be accepted and be able to go there. I learned so much and met some amazing people. I even got students' phone numbers to stay in touch. It was indescribable.

Yes! If Inspire Days comes back, go for it. Don't let that chance pass you because they don't do these things often. Learn from the artists who create impressive films and who are taking time out of their busy movie days to inspire you to one day be in their shoes.

I try not to think that far ahead because in a year, I could change my mind about being in Production and may be in Recruiting or Marketing. I just hope that I'm happy, healthy, and enjoying life.

Q: WHAT IS YOUR DREAM PROJECT?

My dream project would be creating a short film all in stop motion.

Q: WHAT HAS BEEN YOUR PROUDEST MOMENT SO FAR?

My proudest moment will always be getting accepted into DreamWorks, because it solidified my dreams of being in Animation. The hours of driving were tough, but every day there was amazing and well worth it.

Q: WHAT'S THE BEST ADVICE YOU CAN GIVE YOUR PAST SELF, KNOWING WHAT YOU KNOW NOW?

Don't think so much Lily!

Q: ANYTHING YOU'D LIKE TO SHARE?

I have no work that I can share, but I suggest looking up imgur if you're ever feeling down or need a laugh. Sometimes it helps when you're waiting to hear back from a job or an internship.

Q: FAVORITE ANIMATED FILM AND/OR TV SHOW?

Bob's Burgers, Archer, Rick and Morty, ParaNorman, Coraline, Nightmare before Christmas, Big Hero 6, A Bug's Life, Jackie Chan Adventures (JACCCCKIIIIEEEE).

CHAPTER 4

The Interview

The Interview

The interview process is the most intimidating phase for many students. There are tons of variables that come into play and these determine whether you get an offer or not. In this chapter, I'll cover how you'll receive an interview offer, the best way to prepare for both a phone and on-site interview, and the importance of follow up emails.

THE EMAIL

If your application made it to the interview phase, you'll most likely receive an email from the studio's recruiter. It's best practice to respond within 24 hours of receiving the email.

Depending on the recruiter's style, they may ask what your availability is for a phone interview, while others give you various times to choose from. Make sure you respond to the email professionally, providing your availabilities in an easy to read manner.

A PHONE CALL

Sometimes, a recruiter may call you instead of sending an email. On the rare chance that you get a call from a recruiter and you aren't prepared for an interview, you can always let them know you are busy at the moment and ask whether you can reschedule the call for the following day or another time later that week. This will give you time to prepare for the interview.

I had this happened to me on my first internship at Warner Bros. Records. I got a call from a recruiter on my way to class. I eagerly said I had time to talk. Once I realized it was my chance in the music industry, I got nervous and became unsure of my answers. I couldn't articulate and started stuttering words. I realized this, took a deep breath, and was honest with her. I told her "Hey, I'm very nervous and I'm walking between classes. I really want this." She replied, "Don't worry, just answer the best way you can." I went on with the interview. I went to class thinking I blew my chance. About a week later, I received an email from Warner video. If you are in a similar situation, it's better to let the phone call go to voicemail. This way, you'll have more time to prepare for the call.

Prepping For The Interview

I was never great at interviewing. In high school, I was applying for a program and made it to the interview round. It was my first interview ever, and I had no idea what to expect. I was sat in the waiting room among the other hopeful students, and we were all waiting for our names to be called. Once I heard my name, someone escorted me to a room where two interviewers sat. I sat down and they started asking normal questions like "What's your name? What school do you attend?" and so on. Then the questions started getting a bit more difficult. "Why did you apply to this program? Can you tell me about a time when you led a team project and how you led it? What are your strengths and weaknesses?"

By this time, I had no answers but, "I'm a good basketball player. I suck at long distance running." I had nothing. I started sweating really bad. I could tell that the interviewers felt bad for drilling a kid.

I never let this happen to me again. I started to prepare for interviews by writing down my answers and memorizing them. I pretend that I am an actor and I am auditioning for a role as a student intern.

It takes time to prepare and it might make you frustrated, but it will help you develop confidence and prepare better. I've gotten jobs on the spot because of this process. It helped me gain internships and jobs at Warner Bros. Records, Nickelodeon Animation Studio, DreamWorks Animation Studios, Facebook, Google, and Lionsgate.

The way to prepare for interviews is by asking questions that you think they may ask, then writing down your answers and memorizing them. By studying these questions and answers over and over, it will make you more confident. For me, I know how to talk about myself, I pause less, and the words just flow. That's my secret.

The process is a pain in the butt, however, it's always better to be over-prepared than not. It takes a while to answer all these questions for yourself.

After every interview, I still add to my list of questions, improve my answers, and find better ways to articulate my experience.

Opening questions:

1. Tell me about yourself?

2. Can you walk us through your previous work experience?

3. Why do you want to work here?

4. Why are you interested in the production department?

5. Why do you want to be a production intern?

6. Why do you want to work at studio?

7. What do you hope to gain from this experience?

8. What skills are you hoping to gain?

9. Why should we hire you instead of someone else? What can you contribute?

Situational questions:

10. Have you ever had a disagreement? How would you handle that?

11. How do you handle conflict with a co-worker or manager?

12. If you have a project or task due at the end of day and a producer comes up to you asking for help, what do you do?

13. People's personalities can be a bit tough—you have to have thick skin! Have there any been times when you've had to deal with people telling you that you made a mistake, and how do you handle it?

14. How do you deal with difficult people?

15. What did you learn from school or an experience that you can bring to the team?

Organizational questions:

16.   How do you organize your day? How do you stay organized?

17.   How would you handle a high stress situation?

Personality questions:

18.   How would you describe yourself in three words?

19.   What is your biggest pet peeve at work?

20.   Where do you see yourself in 5 years? What are your long-term goals?

21.   What type of work environment do you like to work in?

22.   What type of supervisor do you like to work for?

23.   Describe an experience that changed your life or had a huge impact on your life?

24.   What are three of your strengths?

25.   What are three of your weaknesses?

Previous experience questions:

26.   What excites you the most about work or in your own life?

27.   Give an example of a challenge you faced in your previous job.

28.   Give an example of a mistake you've made in the past. How did you handle it? What did you learn?

29.   Do you prefer a team structure, or do you work better by yourself?

30.   Describe a time when you had to go above and beyond the call of duty? How has this situation affected you?

31.   How do you determine or evaluate success? Give me an example of one of your successful accomplishments? What made you successful?

32.   Has there been a time that you failed? What is your biggest failure?

33.   What has been the greatest obstacle in your life and how has that shaped who you have become today?

34.   Who inspires you? Do you have a role model?

Work habit questions:

35. What do you like the most and the least in your current job?

36. Give an example of suggestions or improvement you've made in a previous work environment.

Team compatibility questions:

37. If we were to talk to your current co-workers, what would they say about you?

38. Give an example of how you solved a problem in a particular project.

39. Tell us about a team project—how did you divide tasks? If you led the team, how did you plan?

Fun questions:

40. If you could make any movie in the world, what movie would you make?

41. What is your favorite film/TV show?

42. What is the worst movie/TV show you've seen and why didn't you like it?

The Phone Interview

Phone interviews are usually only 15 minutes long. It's just a screener and a formality to make sure you are who you say you are, and that you're a good fit for the position so they don't waste the interviewer's time. The questions they ask vary from recruiter to recruiter, but in my experience, I've found that they ask more generic questions.

For example:

- Tell me about your experience (with a specific skill or at a particular company).

- Why do you want to work at this studio?

- Why do you want to intern in this department?

- What are you hoping to gain?

Sometimes they throw in harder questions related to the role:

- How do you organize your day?

- Has there been a time where you've made a mistake and how did you handle it?

For phone interviews, I have a document with all my answers up on my computer screen. By the time the phone rings, I have my hands-free headphones in, leaving my hands ready to scour the document for answers to question they ask. If they like you, they'll set up an on-site interview right then, or via email soon after.

QUESTIONS TO ASK DURING INTERVIEWS

You always need to ask questions at the end of the interview. The interviewer usually asks, "Do you have any questions?" towards the end of the interview. However, even if the interview doesn't ask, you should politely say, "May I ask some questions about the position and the company?" By asking questions, it shows that you've done your research about the company and the position, and that you're interested in the position. Remember, this interview is also for **you** to see whether you like the position and/or company you are interviewing for. You wouldn't want to intern at a place you know you'll dislike. You have to treat it like you are also interviewing them and ask the questions that you really want to know the answers to.

Be wary of their time though. Don't ask too many questions. I'd mix some generic position questions with personal questions about their experience with the company. Research the company and be prepared to ask questions. Due to the 15-minute window of a phone interview, I'd choose three from below. The three most important to me are in bold. If you get an on-site interview, you can ask five-six questions, depending on the time.

GENERIC QUESTIONS:

1. **What would be my primary responsibilities?**

2. How many people work in this department? And what is the culture like?

3. Is this a full-time position with health benefits? And what is the starting pay?

4. What are the hours like and is there a lot of overtime?

5. What is the time frame for filling this role?

1. **When will you be making your final decision?**

1. How would you describe the person that has performed the best in this position? What about them contributed to their success?

2. What would the goals be for the first three months of employment?

3. Can you tell me about any challenges or obstacles I might face?

4. What qualities is the team looking for in a candidate?

PERSONAL QUESTIONS:

Asking personal questions engages the interviewer. Many times, they don't get asked personal questions and in my experience, they are often pleasantly surprised by this. By asking personal questions, you'll more likely be remembered by them, depending how good of a question you ask. It also shows that you have researched them and their career, taking an extra step to prepare for the interview. This is a skill that many companies value.

1. How did you get into this department and how has the studio helped develop your career?

2. Why did you decided to work at the studio rather than their competitors?

3. I noticed you have worked at Studio X before. Why did you leave that studio to work here?

1. **What do you like about working at the studio? And how would you describe the studio's culture?**

THANK YOU NOTES

After you hang up, there is still one more thing you need to do. That is, thank them! Be sure to send a thank you note after a phone or in-person interview. I tend to send them later that same day or at the latest, a day after. With thank you notes, make them short and sweet, thanking them for their time. You should include something that you talked about, or if you forgot to say something, here's your second chance.

Hi (insert name),

Thank you again for setting aside some time to interview me. After hearing more about Pixar and the Production Internship position during our talk, I think being a part of it all would be a unique and rewarding opportunity. It's great to hear that you enjoy working at Pixar very much and it excites me to see how passionate you are about Pixar.

I look forward to hearing back from you in the upcoming weeks.

Best regards,

Eric

On-Site Interview

You'll receive an email if you made it to the in-person interview. Normally, you'll hear back within two weeks, but you should ask when they'll notify you if you made it to an on-site interview during your phone interview. This interview can last anywhere from one to three days for various teams. These aren't full days, but rather are smaller interviews across those days. My Pixar interview was on two different days, meeting with three different teams. My Nickelodeon interview was one day, and it lasted for an hour. DreamWorks was one day, three different teams, and lasted three hours. Warner Bros. Records was one day, two departments, and one hour in total.

DRESS TO IMPRESS

Entertainment is known for its lax work environment with flip flops and shorts, but do not dress how they dress for an interview. You have to stand out. I always wear a suit. I have a blazer with matching slacks, white shirt, black tie, belt, and black dress shoes. I even bring out my watch.

If you don't have a suit, go business casual. Dark slacks, dress shoes, button up dress shirt, and a tie. For ladies, dark slacks or skirts, dress shoes, and a formal blouse.

WHAT TO BRING

Bring a portfolio to write notes-in. Bring a working pen and paper. Carry extra resumes, cover letters, and letters of recommendation from prior work experience.

BE EARLY

Early is on time. On time is late. Late is unheard of! Always be ahead of time. You must also take into consideration parking, finding the office, and checking in.

Make sure to shake hands firmly and be enthusiastic, friendly, and determined. Always keep eye contact and smile. Talk normally, but with confidence and don't use slang.

Once again, be sure to send a thank you note after the interview. If you don't have their contact information, and most likely you won't, then politely ask the recruiter whether they can relay the message.

Hi [recruiter's name],

I hope your day is going well! I was wondering whether you can forward this follow-up email to [interviewer's name] for me?

Hi [interviewer's name],

Thank you again for setting aside some time to interview me. After hearing more about the studio and the Production Internship position during our talk, I feel that being a part of it would be a unique and rewarding opportunity. It's great to hear that you enjoy the Studio very much and it excites me to see how passionate you both are about the production department.

I look forward to hearing back from you in the upcoming weeks.

Best regards,

Eric

If you get a reply such as "Hi Eric, I have sent them your thank you note" from the recruiter, then send a reply saying:

Thank you so much [recruiter's name] for passing along my note and also for setting up the interview!

I hope you have a great date and a wonderful week! ☺

Best regards,

Eric

Q & A With Nicole Rola

- Assistant Animatic Editor at DreamWorks Animation
- Production Coordinator on *Voltron: Legendary Defender* at DreamWorks Animation
- Production Assistant on *Voltron: Legendary Defender* at DreamWorks Animation
- Production Intern on *Steven Universe* at Cartoon Network
- Production Intern on *Lalaloopsy* at Splash Entertainment
- Production Intern on *Legend of Korra* at Nickelodeon Animation Studio

Nicole Rola started as a Production Assistant at DreamWorks Animation. Prior to her animation career, she attended Woodbury University, Burbank, where she got a Bachelor of Fine Arts degree in Animation. As a college student, Nicole landed a couple of awesome internships in the animation industry.

Nicole got her start with Nickelodeon as a Production Intern, where she worked on the hugely popular show *The Legend of Korra*. After her time at Nick, she interned at Cartoon Network as a Production Assistant Intern for the show *Steven Universe*.

Update: After this interview, Nicole was promoted. She is currently an Assistant Animatic Editor at DreamWorks Animation.

Q: WHAT COLLEGE DID YOU ATTEND AND WHAT WAS YOUR MAJOR? DO YOU THINK THIS HELPED WITH YOUR PURSUIT IN THE ENTERTAINMENT INDUSTRY?

I attended Woodbury University, a small private school in Burbank, where I got a Bachelor of Fine Arts degree in Animation. I do think it helped a lot in getting me to where I am now! Nickelodeon was right down the block, which I was stoked about! It was a constant reminder of my goals. The Woodbury internship office also helped a lot with crafting my resume and cover letter.

Q: WHEN DID YOU KNOW YOU WANTED TO BE IN THE

ENTERTAINMENT/ANIMATION INDUSTRY AND WHAT EVENTS LED YOU TO CHOOSE IT?

When I saw a bumper on Nickelodeon showing what it was like to work in their studio, I knew I wanted to work there. I love making people laugh, I love cartoons, and I wanted to love my job. The commercial showed adults playing around like kids and drawing cartoons all day. It didn't look like work—it looked like fun.

Q: DID ANYONE/ANYTHING INSPIRE YOU TO FOLLOW YOUR PASSION FOR ENTERTAINMENT/ANIMATION?

My cousins inspired me to love laughing. Growing up, we were constantly joking around and it felt like a real-life sitcom. I aspired to be as funny as them, come up with the best jokes, and make people smile and laugh. I also loved telling stories, and I loved TV and movies. Emoting experiences through a story is powerful, and finding out that it took many people working together to create this art form made it all the more beautiful. To be a part of that would be my dream.

Q: HOW DID YOU LAND THE INTERNSHIP AT NICKELODEON ANIMATION STUDIO?

As a college freshman, I saw a Nickelodeon booth at an internship fair at school and I freaked out because that was my super childhood dream. I couldn't apply as a freshman, but when I finally became a junior, it was the first thing I worked on. I wrote the craziest cover letter where I pretty much said "IloveSpongebobIloveNickelodeonIloveSpongebob" a million times. I knew I needed help with it, so I asked a Woodbury alum and former Nicktern to read over my cover letter. Thankfully, he helped and said I came off as a fangirl. I revised it to be more professional with just enough fan-girliness to show my personality. I really wanted them to feel how much I wanted to be there.

Q: WHAT WAS THE APPLICATION AND INTERVIEW PROCESS LIKE?

When I was applying in 2013, the HR Nickterns screened the resumes and cover letters, then called the promising ones for phone interviews. I remember waking up to the phone call, half awake, eyes crusty, voice croaky. Be prepared! Friends have also told me where they were caught with the phone interview. It can happen at any time!

Trying to seem as prepared as possible, I answered genuinely with a positive attitude and we hit it off great. My interviewer and I are still friends to this day. Your resume is then passed along to the crew they think you'd fit with. The Production Manager (PM) of that show then calls you to set up an in-person interview. I was as nervous as the dickens, but I think I managed to make a good impression in person.

Q: WHAT DO YOU THINK SET YOUR APPLICATION APART FROM OTHERS?

When interviewing me, the PM confessed he had never read anything like my cover letter before. I had compared my work habits to Spongebob's and even quoted him. "I'm ready! I'm ready!" I was glad he took my letter well, because I wrote a lot of heart into it. It was tough balancing my personality and professionalism, so I was glad it paid off. There are so many capable people trying to get their foot in the door too. To set yourself apart, I think you have to *show who you are.* People want to work with people they can have non-work conversations with, someone who jives with them in a fun way.

Q: ANY ADVICE TO STUDENTS APPLYING TO THE NICKELODEON INTERNSHIP PROGRAM?

My advice is to *be yourself.* They know that every applicant is hard-working, detail-oriented, and other classic resume words. Employers are looking for personalities that fit into their show's culture. People want to work with people they can talk to. With that said, if you don't get accepted, don't give up. There are all types of crews looking for specific kinds of people. And timing is everything. If you keep trying, you increase your chances of getting a yes! You'll never get accepted if you're not there saying "pick me!"

Q: ANY ADVICE TO STUDENTS WHO JUST GOT ACCEPTED INTO THE INTERNSHIP PROGRAM THAT YOU WISH YOU HAD KNOWN?

They say "the whole internship is a job interview," and it really is. Be positive and genuine, **always**. Make **quality connections**, over quantity of connections. Learn as much as you can about everything. Participate and *say yes* to things. If all that sounds scary because you're an introvert, it is. I had to overcome my own shyness to bring out my true self to strangers. A friend told me once that networking is all about being respectful and responsible. Do that and you're golden. Also, when you're there, don't eat a bagel every day! It's free and free is awesome, but bread makes you fat.

Q: WHAT WAS THE INTERNSHIP EXPERIENCE LIKE OVERALL?

It was a dream come true. It was challenging staying upbeat all the time plus juggling school, making a film, and an on-campus job. But I was thankful for every day I was there. It was a truly invaluable experience. Yes, it was scary and difficult, but what worthwhile thing isn't?

Q: YOU INTERNED ON THE SHOW *THE LEGEND OF KORRA*—HOW WAS THAT?

It made me feel very special. I remember my cubicle was right next to industry legends Joaquim Dos Santos and Lauren Montgomery. I looked up to them and was such a fan of their work for so long—it was incredible to be so close to them! I definitely had to hold back my crazy and remind myself that they're just people too. The whole crew was so talented and friendly, I felt very lucky to help out a great team. I got to watch animatics of episodes that hadn't even come out yet! It was torture not to talk about it with my friends, but Korra had two interns and I got to geek out with my intern partner about them!

Q: WHAT WAS THE BEST PART ABOUT BEING A NICKTERN?

Meeting all the cool people! I learned a lot about the process of making an animated TV show, but I also learned a lot about being the best person you can be from a lot of awesome people.

Q: AFTER THE NICKELODEON INTERNSHIP, YOU SCORED AN INTERNSHIP WITH CARTOON NETWORK AS A PRODUCTION ASSISTANT INTERN. WHAT SHOW DID YOU WORK ON AND WHAT DID YOU DO? WAS THERE A DIFFERENCE OF RESPONSIBILITIES BETWEEN THE TWO STUDIOS?

I was lucky enough to intern for *Steven Universe*. The crew was super hard-working and friendly too! The studios differ in personality and structure, and it was a struggle to adjust to the new expectations of Cartoon Network, but in the end, as long as you're respectful and responsible, it's not so different. I had a lot more responsibility on *Steven*, which was great! Internships in general are a great opportunity to meet awesome people and show them you're awesome too!

Q: WHAT WAS THE APPLICATION AND INTERVIEW PROCESS LIKE FOR CARTOON NETWORK?

The process was a little less nerve-wracking since I had done it before. There's an online application where you submit a cover letter and resume, then an in-person interview from a specific show's PM.

Q: WHAT DO YOU THINK SET YOUR APPLICATION APART FROM OTHERS?

What helped me in this case was knowing someone who worked there. My visual development professor at school worked for another Cartoon Network show and he recommended me to the person I interviewed with. People want to work with people they hear good things about—from those they trust. If someone can recommend you, that'll get you far.

Q: ANY ADVICE TO STUDENTS APPLYING TO THE CARTOON NETWORK INTERNSHIP PROGRAM?

Do your research on the show and person you are set to interview with. Really *know* the company; it shows your interest and enthusiasm toward the place and people you want to work with!

Q: ANY ADVICE TO STUDENTS WHO JUST GOT ACCEPTED INTO THE INTERNSHIP PROGRAM THAT YOU WISH YOU HAD KNOWN?

Don't be intimidated if people don't come to you. The Nickternship was more open door and outwardly friendly. At Cartoon Network, the atmosphere is quieter, which may be more intimidating. But once you make an effort to get to know people, everyone is just as friendly. The CN internship doesn't hold your hand—they let you create your own experiences. So, you have to get out there and make those connections and opportunities.

Q: WHAT WAS THE INTERNSHIP EXPERIENCE LIKE AT CARTOON NETWORK OVERALL?

Again, it was a dream come true. I was surrounded by so many talented people, learned about different roles, and how other shows operated. Shows within one studio can have completely different set ups. Talking to other crews is really good, as long as you're keeping up with your responsibilities with your own crew. I got to interview with someone whose position I aspired to have one day, which was priceless information. I also got to show my work to a lot of people during what they call *Intern Pitch Week*. It was scary but liberating to show colleagues what I can do.

Q: NOW, YOU'RE A PRODUCTION ASSISTANT FOR THE TV DIVISION AT DREAMWORKS ANIMATION STUDIOS. WHAT'S THAT LIKE?

Oh my goodness! Have I said it's a dream come true? I work hard on a great show with a team I am proud to be a part of. I learn every day and try to prove myself worthy of being there by bringing my best game to the table.

Q: WHAT ARE THE CULTURAL DIFFERENCES BETWEEN THE THREE MAJOR ANIMATION STUDIOS YOU HAVE WORKED AT: NICKELODEON, CARTOON NETWORK, AND DREAMWORKS?

Nickelodeon was more structured and corporate, but still fun and friendly. Cartoon Network was more cool and reserved, but still open once I took initiative to open doors for myself. DreamWorks is a studio that knows how to work hard and play hard.

Q: WHERE DO YOU HOPE TO BE IN 5 YEARS?

In five years, I hope to be in the animatic editing. I love putting the big picture together and timing things out. Hopefully, animating my own short stuff on the side.

Q: WHAT IS YOUR DREAM PROJECT?

I am working on a dream project! I have a feeling that what I'm helping on will become legendary. Maybe one day, I can experience a comedic, board driven show.

I'm pretty proud of the shorts I helped make in college. There's nothing like being creative with a group of like-minded folks. Seeing a finished film as the synthesis of you and your friends' hard work and passion is a great feeling. I hope I can make more for myself or with a team.

Don't stress out too much. You're not perfect. You're allowed to make mistakes and be you. Don't compare yourself to others, and be in competition with your past self by learning from your mistakes. Everyone is on their own path.

So many… I'll say *Lion King* for film and TV show *Avatar: The Last Airbender*.

Here's a short I did (I need to make more!):

- https://www.youtube.com/watch?v=q-PBQEPbr24

And my lame blog heh:

- http://nicolerola.blogspot.com/

I mostly update my Instagram:

- **@nicolerrola**

CHAPTER 5

The Results

You Got An Offer

Studios usually call if they would like to extend an offer to you and email if you didn't get the position.

If you aren't by your phone, don't worry, as they'll leave a message. If you already got this phone call, then congratulations! All your hard work paid off. After the phone call, they'll send you a confirmation email if you decide to accept the offer. You should reply at the latest within 2 days of receiving the offer. You don't want to play hard to get as they need to make headcount for the program.

SHOULD YOU RELOCATE?

This is only relevant for students who are not local to the studios. I've had many co-interns who relocated from the mid-west, east coast, and myself from Northern California just for an internship opportunity. It's worth the re-location.

We Regret To Inform You

Hey, it happens. I've applied to a bunch of internships and I have been rejected to most of them, many more than I've been accepted into. I've sent the wrong cover letter addressed to a rival studio. I've gotten the silent treatment from my dream company. Despite all of the heartache, this is normal. This is expected, but you have to keep trying until you land one. In order to succeed, you can not let rejection stop you. I kept going and once I started to figure out what these studios looks for, I was able to intern at three major studios in one year!

Most of the time, this rejection is actually for the better. Maybe it wasn't a good culture fit or maybe the role wasn't for you, and you would have been miserable there. That's completely fine. If it doesn't work out, don't be too hard on yourself. There will be other opportunities if you keep trying. Heck, it took me until my fifth year of college to figure this thing out. If you start your search early with this book in hand, you'll have a huge head start.

If you don't get accepted, focus on building your experience and resume to make yourself someone they cannot say no to next time. Keep in touch with all the people you've met, the recruiters, and various interviewers. Now that you've gone through the interview process and have met these people, you are starting to build your network!

If you want to improve yourself for the next time you apply, ask the recruiter whether they have time to explain how to better prepare yourself for the next application and whether they're willing to give you feedback or advice from your interviews. This shows that you are still eager to apply, and if you do happen to improve on those skills next time, they'll take note of it! Recruiters are busy people, so don't expect all of them to set aside time for you. Always be polite when you ask, and try not to sound bitter that you didn't get the internship. Be positive and show that you're in good spirits. This will go a long way.

Pix-Aw

Sometimes, you'll miss out on an internship due to unfortunate events. I've never interned at Pixar, but I have interviewed with them—only to have had bad timing on my side. I was supposed to be a Production Intern on the movie, *The Good Dinosaur*, back in Fall 2013, but at the time Pixar was having problems with the direction of the movie and had to replace the director, in addition to cutting 13% of the company's staff.

I passed the phone interview and three in-person interviews from the Production Assistant to the managers. It was going well. The managers even complimented my work experience and resume saying, "You have quite the resume here."

I received a call back from the recruiter a week after my final interview only to find out that they were not going to run the internship program that quarter. I was speechless. Shocked. Dumbfounded. I didn't know what to say. I thought it was a joke and that they would call me back.

It turned out to be okay, because I ended up interning at DreamWorks Animation in Redwood City on the movie, *Penguins of Madagascar*. This worked out fine for me because I actually took advantage of some of their perks and was able to take a photography class, which developed into a hobby that has let me travel the world capturing iconic landmarks.

After my internship with DreamWorks, I was done with college. Pixar allows you to apply as an intern for six months after graduation, and you bet I did! With DreamWorks, Nickelodeon, and WBR on my resume, I was certain that I was guaranteed an interview. However, they didn't accept me. I reached out to the recruiter who had spoken to me before and she completely forgot about the internship program being canceled the previous semester. I inquired what was wrong with my resume and how I could improve it, to which she answered, "It might not be the resume, it could be a personality fit." But I didn't even get a chance to interview. I concluded that their system had marked me as a "no go" and it stuck with my name. This was and will always be my dream studio to work for.

All in all, I really can't complain. I found a new passion from photography made some great intern friends at DreamWorks, and who knows, if I had gotten that Pixar internship, my Nickelodeon cartoon short, *The Outsiders*, might have never seen the light of day. You can only move forward in a situation like this.

I share this story with you because in this industry, you have to embrace and know that rejection is around the corner and when it happens, keep on moving. Don't let it deter you and your dreams. Let it fuel your passion to do better. Everyone has their own path and you should choose to embrace it, no matter what it is.

Q & A With Nancy Covarrubias

- Production Coordinator on *Rise of Teenage Mutant Ninja Turtles* at Nickelodeon Animation Studio
- Social Media Short Production Coordinator on *Pinky Malinky* at Nickelodeon Animation Studio
- Production Coordinator on *Dora & Friends: Into the City!* at Nickelodeon Animation Studio
- Production Assistant on *Dora & Friends: Into the City!* at Nickelodeon Animation Studio
- Production Intern on *T.U.F.F Puppy/The Fairly OddParents* at Nickelodeon Animation Studio

Nancy Covarrubias attended Woodbury University in Burbank, CA, eventually earning an Animation/Fine Arts degree. Shortly after graduating, Nancy made her animation debut working on one of the toughest shows in children's television, *Dora And Friends: Into the City!* However, her journey was no walk in the park. Like many other students trying to break into the animation industry, she had to overcome the challenges and competitiveness that comes with the industry.

But she didn't let this get her down. Instead, she used this as motivation and a helpful resource to figure out what these animation internship programs were looking for. With the help of her peers, Nancy reworked her cover letter and resume and was offered an incredible internship opportunity with Nickelodeon Animation Studios to work on both of Butch Hartman's shows, *The Fairly OddParents* and *T.U.F.F Puppy*.

Update: Since this interview, Nancy is currently working as a Production Coordinator on the show, *Rise of Teenage Mutant Ninja Turtles*.

Q: WHAT DO YOU DO?

I'm a Production Assistant on a Preschool show that airs on Nick Jr. The show I work on is called *Dora and Friends: Into the City!* The show is a spin-off of *Dora The Explorer* and it involves some of Dora's new and old friends going on adventures in the city. On the show, I oversee the storyboard department, so I do a lot of note-taking for the artists during meetings, making sure all the board artists are on track and have the most up to date materials to work on a particular sequence on an episode.

Q: WHEN DID YOU KNOW YOU WANTED TO BE IN THE ANIMATION/ENTERTAINMENT INDUSTRY AND WHAT EVENTS LED YOU TO CHOOSE IT?

Growing up, I always loved drawing and anything to do with art. It was my favorite subject! I knew from a very young age that I wanted to become an artist or do something that involved art.

Q: DID ANYONE/ANYTHING INSPIRE YOU TO FOLLOW YOUR PASSION FOR ANIMATION/ENTERTAINMENT?

In college, there were days when I just felt like giving up because I thought my art wasn't good enough. My professors were always motivating students, but sometimes that wasn't enough. What really helped me was my peers. A lot of them were landing really cool internships and I wasn't. Instead of feeling bad about that, I had my college friends look at my resume and cover letter for feedback and tips. My friends in college were a good source of motivation. They told me to just keep applying and have patience. It did take me a few tries until I was able to land the Nick internship.

Q: SO YOU STARTED OFF AS A PRODUCTION INTERN AT NICKELODEON ANIMATION STUDIOS FOR *THE FAIRLY ODDPARENTS*—HOW WAS THAT?

I first interned on *T.U.F.F. Puppy* and soon found myself assisting *The Fairly OddParents* production crew too. I really wanted to learn as much as I could about production, so I asked the coordinators on *The Fairly OddParents* whether they needed an extra hand and they were very cool about it. So I was lucky to have helped both production crews.

Q: WHAT WAS IT LIKE INTERNING ON *T.U.F.F. PUPPY*?

I felt lucky to have interned on such an awesome crew. Everyone was very friendly and so down to earth. I was kind of quiet and shy when I first interned, but the crew always invited me out to lunch with them and made me feel like I was really part of the crew. The show's creator, Butch Hartman, would have what he called a "T.U.F.F. Puppy pitch" or a "Fairly Odd Pitch," where his production crews would sit and hear him pitch an episode that his team of writers created. He assembled a quick animatic and read the script in the character's voices. This was my favorite experience of my internship.

Q: WHAT WAS THE APPLICATION AND INTERVIEW PROCESS LIKE WHEN APPLYING TO THE INTERNSHIP PROGRAM?

During the time that I applied, I don't remember there being an application process. I do remember going online to the Nickelodeon career page and they had an email address where people could submit their resume and cover letter. When I was in college, I submitted my resume and cover letter probably four or five times. I remember feeling discouraged because I wasn't getting any calls or emails. Manny Grijalva, who was my college peer, had recently gotten hired at Nick. So he helped me out a lot through the submission process. He told me that if I had any questions, to just ask him. After sending him my resume and cover letter for feedback, I resent my stuff to Nickelodeon and not too long after that, I landed my first interview with *T.U.F.F. Puppy*!

Q: WHAT DO YOU THINK SET YOUR APPLICATION/INTERVIEW APART FROM OTHERS?

I was very honest and enthusiastic in my interview, and I think they picked up on that. They really liked that I had a background in animation and was looking forward to learning about production. Dasha Khailova, who was production manager on *T.U.F.F. Puppy* at the time, asked me about my past experiences, so I told her about my part-time job working as an art instructor at a recreational area. I was working with kids aged 4-15 years old and teaching them about animation, what a character expression sheet was, and what a character line-up was. Dasha was sort of surprised that I was teaching young kids about animation. She liked that I was excited to teach these kids about art. I believe that made me stand out among the other candidates they were interviewing.

Q: WHAT WAS THE INTERNSHIP EXPERIENCE LIKE OVERALL?

I loved my internship experience at Nick. I especially liked that I was a part of two separate production crews and I got to learn so much about the animation pipeline.

Q: WHAT WAS THE BEST PART ABOUT BEING A NICKTERN?

The best part of the internship was that the studio organized fun activities for the interns such as "Game Night" and every Friday, we had "Nicktern Screenings." The screenings were awesome because the interns would get to spend an hour watching cartoon classics while eating popcorn and candy, and drinking soda! Not many people at other companies or internships can say they did that at work. I had a blast!

Q: ANY ADVICE TO STUDENTS APPLYING TO THE NICKELODEON INTERNSHIP PROGRAM?

The advice I'd give to anyone trying out for the Nick internship is to work hard, stay on top of your tasks, take lots of notes, but don't forget to have fun. It goes by really fast, so make time to meet up with your internship peers and plan one-on-one meetings with artists or production people at the studio. If you're an aspiring artist, don't be afraid to show your work. Most artists at the studio are more than happy to critique and give feedback. It's a great opportunity to have a professional look at your work, so don't let that go to waste while interning. I also recommend shadowing people, if they are okay with it of course. I shadowed my *T.U.F.F. Puppy* PA for a while and took notes as I watched her do breakdowns. I wanted to just absorb everything like a sponge, so that I'd be prepared for a PA position if a job opened up.

Q: BUTCH HARTMAN HAS AN AMAZING ANIMATION BACKGROUND TO HIS NAME WHAT WAS IT LIKE WORKING WITH HIM ON *THE FAIRLY ODDPARENTS*?

Butch Hartman is really cool. I kind of wish I'd got to interact with him a lot more during my internship, but he's a pretty busy guy. I only got to talk to him briefly a couple of times. But I like that he's the type of show creator who really knows what he wants. He's been working at Nickelodeon for many years, so his shows are like a well-oiled machine.

Q: AFTER YOUR INTERNSHIP WITH NICKELODEON, YOU SCORED A PRODUCTION ASSISTANT POSITION ON THE SHOW *DORA & FRIENDS*. WHAT DOES YOUR DAY-TO-DAY LOOK LIKE?

My day-to-day on Dora is pretty busy most of the time. I got hired on Dora not knowing much about a Preschool show's pipeline, but I quickly learned that it was very different than working on *The Fairly OddParents* and *T.U.F.F. Puppy*. One major comparison between Butch Hartman's shows and working on a Preschool show like Dora is that Butch skips the Animatic part of the pipeline. On Dora, the Animatic is really important because our New York crew has researchers who use the Animatic for testing and see how children respond to the show.

On a day-to-day, I'll sit in script meetings, thumbnail board meetings, etc. I'll even sit with the Producer and Animatic Editor as they review the Animatic. Every time the Producer calls out a revision note, I'll make sure to pass that information to the Revisionists. I also keep track of the Board Artists and make sure they have work, and are referencing the most up to date materials for that given episode. And I help keep track of deadlines and make sure the Board Artist and Directors know about upcoming meetings. On our show, we have tons of meetings! Each meeting sometimes runs to about 2-3 hours. Half of our Dora & Friends crew is on the east coast, so we'll do video conference calls with the show creators and team in New York.

Q: HOW DID YOU MAKE THE TRANSITION FROM AN INTERN TO A FULL-TIME EMPLOYEE AT NICKELODEON?

The transition from intern to full-time Production Assistant was exciting for me. It had been a dream of mine to work for Nickelodeon. It wasn't a big adjustment other than the working hours. I found myself working many late nights on Dora due to it being a brand new show, and Production was still trying to figure out the pipeline in Season One. But it was really interesting being there at the start of the show and seeing how Production built its pipeline and how much has changed since Season One.

Q: WHERE DO YOU HOPE TO BE IN 5 YEARS?

In five years, I'd still like to be working in the Animation industry. I really have a passion for cartoons, so I think Animation is the career for me. I'd hope to have transitioned to an artist position, such as Revisionist or Color Stylist.

Q: WHAT IS YOUR DREAM PROJECT?

My dream project would be to work on a pitch with a close friend, and actually have it green lighted for a series. That's probably my ultimate dream.

Q: WHAT HAS BEEN YOUR PROUDEST MOMENT SO FAR?

My proudest moment would have to be getting hired at Nick. I'm grateful I was given this opportunity and have been able to work with such a talented team on Dora.

Q: WHAT'S THE BEST ADVICE YOU CAN GIVE YOUR PAST SELF, KNOWING WHAT YOU KNOW NOW?

If I were to go back in time and give myself advice, I'd probably tell myself to do more internships in college. I had so much fun during my Nick internship that I wished I'd applied to more internships. I would have gained more experience and knowledge if I had made time in my schedule back then. The best thing you can do while in college is apply for internships, because often times your internship experience can open doors for job opportunities and networking. So the more work experience you have, the better opportunities you get.

Q: FAVORITE ANIMATED FILM AND/OR TV SHOW?

My favorite animated TV show has to be a Nick classic of course. I love *Hey Arnold!* I own the complete series! And I got the chance to meet Hey Arnold's show creator, Craig Bartlett, while in college. He's really nice and even signed my DVD box set!

CHAPTER 6

You're An Intern, Now What?

The Life Of An Intern

You are now about to enter the longest job interview of your life…and I don't mean to be so dramatic, but the life of an intern is a constant balance of learning, working, and enjoying the moment. It can be tough juggling all of that while trying to make a good, long-lasting impression in the hopes of getting hired.

The life of an intern can be stressful at times, but it can also be fun. Embrace it, and enjoy the ups and downs. Trust me, internships go by fast—and soon you'll be yearning for this time again.

It's not an easy feat adjusting to the working world, while learning new skills, trying to make a good impression, and worrying about school. Just know, internships are meant to be a **learning ground**, so you can fail hard now rather than later in your professional life. In this section, I'll go over the best way to get the most out of your internship, both professionally and socially. But first, you need to get your mindset right.

Get Your Mindset Right

Get your mindset right. Get your mindset right. Get your mindset right. This is so important. Before you even step foot into that studio, you must get your mindset right. You have to understand that this is a place of trying, where the learning curve is high, and mistakes are bound to happen. Still, strive to be the best version that you can be and get out of your comfort zone. But don't be so determined to make a good impression that you sabotage every other intern who gets in your way. There's plenty of work for everyone. Be nice, be friendly, work hard, and enjoy what you do.

DRESS THE PART

Nickelodeon really ingrains this in their interns. They came up with the phrase, "This is the longest job interview of your life, so dress the part."

The point of dressing up is to **stick out**. It's to let the employees know that you are an intern who is taking this internship seriously. You don't need to wear a suit or a dress every day, but always dress business-casual. For men, wear dress pants or nice slacks, a button up shirt, a tie, and dress shoes. For women, wear dress pants or a long skirt, a button up shirt or a nice blouse, and dress shoes or nice flats.

I always dressed up in a tie. As the program progresses, some interns get comfortable and start to dress more relaxed. There was one time at Nickelodeon when the VP of Nick walked into our class. He looked around and noticed that I was the only one wearing a tie and said, "You look sharp. How come the rest of you guys aren't dressed up?" I was eventually able to set up a meeting with him to pick his brain. It never hurts to look good. It shows your professionalism and how seriously you are taking this opportunity.

EXCEED EVERYONE'S EXPECTATIONS

During my DreamWorks internship, we had a chance to sit down with Jeffrey Katzenberg, Founder and CEO of DreamWorks. Someone asked him what was the best advice he could give to an intern, and he said, "Exceed everyone's expectations."

This stuck with me. It's simple. If someone asks you to photocopy something, you make sure you make the best damn photocopy that they've ever seen in the quickest time. People take notice when you work extra hard, even for the smallest task.

DON'T BE ANNOYING

Don't be that intern who bothers everyone and asks a question every five minutes just for the sake of asking a question. You have to learn when to ask questions for work and when to be a self-starter. Also, don't actively seek praise for your work. When interns do this, they lose focus on the task at hand. If you've been doing great work for the company, I'm sure the company will take notice and will reward you appropriately. Let your work speak for itself and the rest will follow.

SHADOWING

If you want to learn more about a role in the company, then shadowing is a great way to get first-hand experience and learn what someone does in their job. If you want to find out more about a specific role, you should ask your supervisor whether they'll allow you to take some time away from your duties to shadow someone. Then, reach out to the person you would like to shadow and ask them whether they would be okay with it. If they agree, bring a pen and a notepad with you to take notes of what their daily job involves. After you are done shadowing, send them an email thanking them for their time, and thank your supervisor for letting you take the opportunity.

BUILD YOUR NETWORK

An internship is your opportunity to meet and connect with industry professionals on a personal level. Some internships, like Nickelodeon, encourage you to set up meetings with an employee who works in your field of interest.

How to Set up a Meeting

E-mail: Be polite and be aware of their busy schedule. Don't assume they are free to meet you.

What to Bring and How to Act in a Networking Meeting

1. Research the person beforehand, and prepare a couple of questions to ask them.

2. Ask questions to start the conversations and then let it flow naturally. Remember, **listening** is just as important as speaking.

3. Be cautious of their time and don't let the meeting run too long. If you think they have work to get back to, it's nice to always say, "I don't want to take up too much of your time," and see how they respond.

KEEPING IN CONTACT

After you meet with someone, send a follow up e-mail thanking them. You can include topics that you discussed during the meeting to show that you were engaged.

To keep in contact, send emails periodically to check in and see how they are doing during your internship and even after the program commences. Every 3-6 months is appropriate for checking in. Don't send these emails too often, as it can be annoying and rub them the wrong way.

LETTER OF RECOMMENDATION

When your internship is coming to an end, and if you feel you did a great job and built a connection with your supervisor, then you can ask for a letter of recommendation. This will help you in future internships and jobs, as it builds your credibility and provides information that is not on your resume or cover letter—from a supervisor who has worked with you.

If your supervisor says no, then ask them for feedback. Sometimes companies don't allow supervisors to give out letters of recommendation. If this is the case, ask whether you can use them as a reference for future employment opportunities. If they agree, exchange email addresses to keep in contact.

Q & A With Tiffany Chiu

- Production Coordinator on *She-Ra and the Princesses of Power* at DreamWorks Animation

- Production Assistant on *The Dawn of the Croods* at DreamWorks Animation

- Executive Assistant on *Legend of Korra* at Nickelodeon Animation Studio

- Production Intern on *Legend of Korra* at Nickelodeon Animation Studio

After scoring a Production internship with Nickelodeon Animation Studio, Tiffany Chiu quickly worked her way into one of the biggest animated TV shows of 2014, *The Legend of Korra*, where she worked closely with none other than the creators of the show, Bryan Konietzko and Michael Dante DiMartino.

Before her time on *The Legend of Korra*, Tiffany, like many other talented students, had no idea how to break into the animation industry. She had always enjoyed watching cartoons, drawing, and pretty much anything that involved creativity, but it wasn't until high school when she found out that she could do this for a living. Tiffany's SAT teacher told her of a friend who was a designer and worked on *Star Wars*.

"[H]e opened my eyes to the many opportunities available to work as an artist in the industry."

With this new ambition and determination to break into the animation industry, Tiffany decided to study at California State University of Fullerton and received a BFA in Animation before making her animation career debut at Nickelodeon Animation Studio.

Update: Since the interview, Tiffany is currently working as a Production Coordinator at DreamWorks Animation on *She-ra and the Princesses of Power*.

Q: YOU STARTED OFF AS AN INTERN FOR NICKELODEON. HOW DID YOU FIND OUT ABOUT NICKELODEON'S INTERNSHIP PROGRAM AND WHAT WAS THE APPLICATION PROCESS LIKE?

I found out about the internship when I was a member of our school's animation club called Pencil Mileage Club. The application process was very simple. I just submitted my resume and a cover letter online, but I didn't hear back about an interview until a month later. Nickelodeon gets thousands of resumes, so I knew it would take a while.

Q: AS A NICKTERN, WHAT DEPARTMENT WERE YOU A PART OF AND WHAT DID A TYPICAL DAY LOOK LIKE FOR YOU?

I was a Production Intern on *The Legend of Korra* during the Fall 2013 term. A typical day for me was to provide assistance to my production manager or producer with various tasks. After I finished all the assigned tasks, I would ask around to see whether any other members on the show needed my assistance. Occasionally, I would attend classes and fun special events offered as a part of the internship program. In my spare time, I would often schedule meetings or interviews with employees I wanted to meet to learn more about the experience of the people working in the industry.

Q: WHAT WAS THE INTERNSHIP EXPERIENCE LIKE OVERALL?

It was awesome. There's no other way to describe it. I met so many people, made new friends, and learned so much about the animation industry. It only made my passion and knowledge in animation grow.

Q: ANY ADVICE TO STUDENTS APPLYING TO NICKELODEON?

Your resume and cover letter are really important. Ask your friends, classmates, and/or family members for feedback on them. It's very important to understand that it's okay to ask for help when needed. You should always have the same attitude in a work environment, because it's better to ask for help than to act like you know what you are doing and end up making a mistake.

Q: HOW IS THE CULTURE AT NICKELODEON?

Everyone is super friendly and we all have the same desire to produce nothing but the best, and Nickelodeon will always continue to maintain it that way.

Q: HOW DID YOU MAKE THE TRANSITION FROM AN INTERN TO A FULL-TIME EMPLOYEE AT NICKELODEON?

As my college career and internship were both coming to an end, luckily a position for an Executive Assistant on *The Legend of Korra* became available. My team members encouraged me to pursue this opportunity; I immediately applied for it and was accepted. I was fortunate that the opportunity came up when I needed it. In most cases, getting a job in this industry requires much patience.

Q: YOU BECAME AN EXECUTIVE ASSISTANT FOR *THE LEGEND OF KORRA*! THAT MUST HAVE BEEN AN EXCITING SHOW TO WORK ON?

It was super exciting and definitely a once in a lifetime experience. To this day, I am still amazed I got the opportunity to work on that show. I have been a big *Avatar: The Last Airbender* fan for as long as I can remember and getting the chance to work with the creators of that show was a huge learning curve for me and a great step into the animation industry. The experience definitely opened my eyes to TV animation production in a way I had never viewed it before.

Q: WHAT CAN SOMEONE EXPECT TO DO AS AN EXECUTIVE ASSISTANT?

Basically, manage the executive's calendars, take messages, and coordinate meetings. In a nutshell, being proactive as administrative support to the top executives and the team.

Q: HOW WAS WORKING WITH THE SHOW'S CREATORS, BRYAN KONIETZKO AND MICHAEL DANTE DIMARTINO?

Bryan and Mike are great people to work with. I never felt like my job was one of those typical assistant jobs where I just did whatever the boss told me to do. They treated me and everyone else on the team with equal respect. I felt like I was helping them with the workload and pressure they constantly had, rather than just doing my "job," and I was very happy doing it. They were not only my bosses, but also my mentors and I learned so much from working with such respected individuals in the industry.

Q: WAS *THE LEGEND OF KORRA* A TOUGH SHOW TO WORK ON?

I don't think "tough" is the best word to describe it. Although the project was challenging at all levels (pre-production to post-production), seeing the final product made the experience well worth the effort. Everyone on the team was like family; we helped each other in times of need.

Q: WHAT IS YOUR FAVORITE ANIMATED FILM AND/OR TV SHOW?

I love too many animated films and shows. But my top picks would be *Finding Nemo*, *Gargoyles* (Disney TV Series), *Foster's Home for Imaginary Friends*, and *Avatar: The Last Airbender*.

Q: DID ANYONE OR ANYTHING INSPIRE YOU TO FOLLOW YOUR PASSION FOR ANIMATION?

Oh man…all of the artists/creators behind my favorite animated movies and television series are huge inspirations. Also, all of my college art instructors and co-workers are definitely inspirations for my passion. They all showed me that being able to bring out your creativity and imagination to life for the world to see is something very inspiring and something I would love to be a part of.

Q: WHERE DO YOU HOPE TO BE IN 5 YEARS?

To be character designing for an animated feature film or animated television series.

Q: WHAT IS YOUR DREAM PROJECT?

Definitely to create and produce my own animated show. But getting the opportunity to character design for an animated film is already a dream to me.

Q: WHAT HAS BEEN YOUR PROUDEST MOMENT?

Seeing my name in the end credits as part of the team who brought this great show to such a wide audience was one of the most satisfying moments in my career.

CHAPTER 7

Turning Your Internship Into Something Bigger

How I Went From Intern To Cartoon Creator At Nickelodeon

Once you have gained an internship, you need to take advantage of it and try to turn it into an opportunity for something bigger. I did this by turning my internships into being a cartoon creator. So, in the final chapter, I'll show you how to turn your internship into something bigger. First, I'll tell you how I became a cartoon creator, to show you it is possible despite any doubts you might have. I'll tell you some of the mistakes I made on my journey, so you can hopefully avoid them. Then I'll give you some final tips.

I first heard about Nickelodeon's Animated Shorts Program when I was an intern there back in Spring 2013. There were tons of flyers on bulletin boards and advertisements on the lobby's TV screen. It was open to the public, so you didn't have to be a Nickelodeon employee or intern to apply at the time. (Today, I believe they have made the Shorts Program exclusive to only Nickelodeon affiliates.) Most of our intern class was going to pitch. It was a big thing amongst us. I think we all wanted to pitch something just so we could go back home and brag to our friends and family about how we pitched a cartoon to Nickelodeon!

Initially, I wanted to work with an artist, since I can't draw to save my life. But all the artistic interns had already formed a group or didn't want to pitch. Two of my department co-interns were going to write and pitch a script and one of them was going to pitch a pre-school one. The writers asked me whether I wanted to join, but I decided to pitch by myself.

My supervisor told me that *Adventure Time* was once a Nickelodeon short, but Nick passed on it and now they were kicking themselves in the butt, which was why they started the Animated Shorts Program again. He said he thought they were looking for a similar type of show—a buddy comedy duo geared towards boys. As I started to come up with an idea for a short, I had no clue where to start. I've never written anything in my life, besides school papers. My co-intern, who was pitching the pre-school program, gave me some great advice. He said, "Write something that you would want to see on TV." Once that manifested in my head, I went home and started to write. Every night, I would watch *Regular Show, Impractical Jokers*, and I started getting into *Community*. I wanted my script to be raunchy like *The Ren & Stimpy Show*. I would binge watch these shows, then open up my Word document and start writing my own script. The key to making it funny was if it made me laugh. If I thought of a joke that just had me laughing out loud, I would include it.

It was getting close to the end of my internship, and close to the pitch deadline, so I sent an email to the person in charge to set up a meeting. I choose a meeting the very last week that I could, so I could continue to write and make my short better. The pitch day came and I was a mess. I forgot to fill out the submission release form, so I was scrambling around to get it printed, completed, and stapled together. Of course, in true comedy style, I picked the broken stapler, which left the staple sticking out ready to stab somebody. My writing was barely legible, and I rushed to the meeting room huffing and puffing.

When I walked in, I saw two executives, one being the founder of Nickelodeon Animation. They seemed tired and exhausted from listening to pitches all day. I walked towards the table with a character description page, three copies of my script, and the f**ked up release form. They told me to sit down. Then they asked about my background. I explained that I was a Managerial Economics major, essentially just a Business major, from UC Davis and that I was interning in the Vault department. I could see their eyes roll a bit when I said I was from the Vault. The Vault wasn't the most glamorous internship position in the eyes of some, but I loved it!

They asked what I had for them and I said I just had a script and a description of the characters. Slightly impatient, one of them asked me whether I just wanted to read the script. That was the plan all along in my head. Nervously, I began to read the script in a very monotone voice. By the start of the second page, I heard a laugh. I kept reading. Then I heard another laugh. I kept reading and then I heard an even louder laugh. At this point, I felt pretty good about my script. My confidence was increasing as they kept laughing. By the end of the 10 pages, they had tears in their eyes. They giggled and related personal experiences to my story. Then one of the executives, Mary, looked me straight in the eye and asked me whether we wanted to make this short. I was shocked. I felt elated. I was so happy. Of course I wanted to make this! They gave me some notes and I wrote them all down. They asked me whether I could re-write the script with their notes and send it their way when I was done so they could bring it to the higher ups.

I left that room with the biggest smile on my face. I had no idea what just happened. I was still in shock that they liked my script. The very first script that I had ever written in my life. After work, on my way home, I called my mom to tell her how it went. I don't think she really understood, and I think she thought every intern experienced that. When I got back to my apartment, I opened my laptop and just stared at the script. Now the hard part. What do I change? Do I even agree with their notes? How can I improve this script?

The executives had sent me a script of another show, so I could format mine correctly. That's right, I had just written the script in a Word document with the names in bold, a semi-colon, and then hit the return bar. I studied the script intensely to learn how to format correctly. I eventually added a funny scene and implemented some of their feedback. I sent the updated script to them. A week later, I had to leave my internship mid-program to go back to school to start my Spring Quarter. I really didn't want to be in school. Here I was, on the verge of getting a cartoon short made with Nickelodeon, and I was in class learning about agriculture business. I really couldn't focus. A month passed. I got an email from one of them with unfortunate news. She said I should be proud as my script reached executive level, but they were going to have to pass on it. I was devastated.

A year later, I graduated and finished my internship with DreamWorks Animation. I went on a three-week trip to Japan as my post-graduation getaway. During my trip, I received an email from the coordinator of the Nickelodeon Shorts Program asking whether I'd be open to pitching again. I jumped at the opportunity and set up a time. When I got back home, I was determined to write a better script. I came up with one idea that I ended up working on for two months. I knew it wasn't going anywhere. The pitch was a week away when I decided to just pitch my previous short again. I figured that if they liked it once, they'd love it this time with the jokes being beefed up even more.

The week of the pitch, I had a feeling that I needed something else. I had nothing. It was a Tuesday and my pitch meeting was on Thursday. Then all of a sudden, as I was staring at a blank document, I got an idea. I felt like I vomited these words, stories and jokes out. I was thinking so quickly that my hands couldn't type fast enough. An hour later, *The Outsiders* was born in 10 full pages. I showed it to my brother and he loved it. I showed it to my girlfriend and she loved it. She even added a joke! I had a great feeling about the pitch meeting.

I drove to Los Angeles from San Francisco for the meeting. I had two shorts in hand. My old one and *The Outsiders*. I added a lot more jokes to the first script, and I didn't add anything to *The Outsiders*. I got to the meeting dressed in a sports coat and a tie. The shorts coordinator complimented my attire (which is why you should always dress to impress). I read the first script to her and didn't get much of a reaction. I thought that was strange. But then I read *The Outsiders*, and she was laughing half-way down the first page. She ended up laughing so hard that she started to tear up. I had to stop reading or she wouldn't have heard what happens next. She had just eaten pizza too, so her hands had some grease on, which got in her eye and made her cry even more! We both laughed about that. She absolutely loved the script and was super excited to show it to everyone else. A month later, I got a call saying that they wanted to make my short! This led to the 2-year development of *The Outsiders*.

This story goes to show that the path to success isn't always smooth, but it is possible. If there are any lessons to take from this experience, any advice I can give you knowing what I know now, it's this:

- **Take your opportunities** when they come up. Getting to pitch a short to Nickelodeon isn't something that comes up every day, so leap at those chances when they're offered.

- Don't be put off trying for something if you think you don't have the skills needed. Sometimes those skills aren't as important as you think they are. If you want to be in animation but you can't draw, it doesn't mean you won't be amazing. **Just give it a go!**

- Speak to other people if you're struggling for ideas or need help with something. **Talking to other people** can be a huge help. My friend and my supervisor really helped me. Don't be afraid to ask other people for input.

- **Preparation** is really important. I nearly messed up my pitch because I wasn't fully prepared. Read any submission or application processes thoroughly before you apply. Prepare in plenty of time.

- At some points in life, rejection is inevitable, for whatever reason. <u>Don't let it get you down if you're rejected</u>, and if you really want it, keep trying. Apply again next time.

- **Always try to improve**. When I went back to Nick with my original pitch, it didn't have the same effect. But my new script did. You should always be trying to improve yourself.

- **Dress to impress**. It shows you're willing to go the extra mile to be noticed, and it makes you look professional and serious about the opportunity.

Say Yes, Then Decide Later

The Nickelodeon internship was my favorite internship of the three by far, but it almost didn't happen. In this section, I'll tell you how I got the internship and the mistakes I made, so you can avoid them on your journey.

The Nickelodeon internship program was ranked in the top 10 internships by Forbes for a reason. The whole process—from applying to interviewing to the program itself—was thoroughly thought-out, and you could sense how much Nick value their interns.

During my time there, I felt very proud of being a Nicktern and it was hard to leave the building at the end of the day. My intern class bonded well, often going out to Barney's in downtown Burbank to hang out. The employees and staff treat you with respect and never once make you feel like an intern whose main purpose is to get coffee. If you are interning in a department that you may not like, the studio encourages you to set up meetings with other employees in different departments to ask inquisitive questions. They are also open to you switching careers.

However, I could have missed out on all of this. In fact, explaining how I got my internship at Nickelodeon is a story that makes me cringe still to this day.

I pushed my graduation date after I got my internship at Warner Bros. Records, and it was pushed again after my Nickelodeon internship. The problem was, I was really anxious about graduating at the time, and I just wanted to get my degree already. At this point, I hadn't been in school actually pursing my degree for about a year. I was so close, and I was afraid that I wasn't going to graduate if I accepted the internship at Nick.

I applied to the Nickelodeon internship program during my WBR internship and got an interview. After the interview, I got a call that I had been accepted into the program! I was super excited, as it was my dream to work there, but when the recruiter asked whether I was still interested in the program,

I hesitated. School was in the back of my mind. I asked whether I could let him know my decision later in the week. He said "Sure, no problem, but remember that this position and the acceptance might not be honored if you apply again the following semester." Later, he confessed that he'd never had someone put the offer on hold—I don't recommend doing this at all! A few days later, I made my decision. At that moment, my mind was set. I wasn't going to take the offer. I called them and the phone rang. And rang. And went to answering machine. Lucky me.

A couple of hours later, I had time to reconsider my decision and thought school can wait! When Nickelodeon called me back, I accepted the offer. It was the best decision I've ever made. The internship was the most fun I had. I met some of the coolest people. I was surrounded by assets from Nickelodeon's 90's classics on a daily basis. On top of all of that, I ended up making a cartoon short with Nickelodeon. I'm happy as hell that they didn't answer my first call, and I'm grateful that I came to my senses.

If there's anything to be learned from this experience, it might sound crazy, but **<u>never let school get in the way of your education</u>**.

You will learn so much at an internship, and will have so many amazing experiences. You'll meet people who might offer you your next career opportunity, and you'll get the chance to build a network in the industry. So when you're given that opportunity, don't pass it up, don't hesitate like I did, and please don't put the offer on hold!

This story could have gone awry. They might have said no when I asked for more time to reconsider. They might have picked up the phone when I called to say I wasn't taking it. I was lucky, but it's not worth taking that risk.

If you get an opportunity to intern somewhere like Nickelodeon, and it's your dream, don't let the opportunity pass you by. School can wait—it will still be there after your internship. But the internship probably won't wait. Take the opportunity when it's presented to you, because it might just be the best thing you ever do!

Final Words

Now that you know my story and how I was able to land three internships in one year—turning it into a career that I could only dream of—it is your turn to do the same. I've had my share of rejections. I've made many mistakes on the journey. But I didn't let this deter me from my goal. I started to learn and continued to grow, because I was determined to reach my goal and was persistent about it. If you want an animation internship, you can get it! You just have to work for it. You have all of the necessary knowledge to get one, so there are no excuses.

Now that you've seen my cover letters and the resumes that got me the various internships, use this information and knowledge to your advantage. Remember, I can only help so much, but it is ultimately up to you and how determined you are. I provided you with my blueprint so that you can learn from and utilize it for yourself.

A few key things to take away. Remember to apply every chance that you get. Once you hit your third-year status (if you took an AP course or summer classes, you might get there sooner), start to apply to every studio, every semester. Summer months are the most competitive. Consider applying during the off-season months of Fall and Spring. Be open-minded and apply beyond the animation industry. There's really no reason for you not to. During your first and second year, start building up resume experience that a recruiter can't say no to.

I have faith that if you stay consistent and determined, and are always improving your experience, then you will land an internship. If there's something that I didn't mention in this book, or if you have any questions or comments, feel free to visit my website at www.eric-bravo.com and send me a short, brief email or message.

If you'd like me to review your resume or cover letter, or would like to have some office hours with me, I provide these services for a fee. If you're interested, you can find the services on my website or email me with a relevant heading. It warms my heart when someone asks for my help to land an internship. My goal for this book is to help as many people as I can. If this book helped you, or if you landed an internship, drop me a line too, as I'd love to hear about it!

I will end this book with words that Jeffery Katzenberg gave me...a way of living that I try to live by everyday:

"Exceed everyone's expectation, no matter how small or big the task it. If you are asked to make a photocopy, make it the best damn photocopy that you've ever made and delivery it the quickest."

Q & A With Bettina Braganza

- Event Marketing Manager at Nickelodeon Animation Studio
- Event Marketing Coordinator at Nickelodeon Animation Studio
- Special Events Intern at Nickelodeon Animation Studio
- Creative Licensing/Video Production Intern at Sony Music Entertainment

Bettina Braganza has one of the coolest jobs in the animation industry. Besides being the official tour guide of Nickelodeon Animation Studio, she helps plan out Nickelodeon's Kid's Choice Awards, Comic Con, and premiere parties for various Nickelodeon shows. Bettina graduated from UC Irvine with a degree in Business Economics. She always knew she wanted to be in entertainment, but had no idea what industry exactly.

After landing an internship with Nickelodeon as an Event Marketing Intern, Bettina developed a love for the animation industry. She became the Event Marketing Assistant shortly after the internship ended.

Update: Since this interview, Bettina is currently working as an Event Marketing Manager.

Q: WHEN DID YOU KNOW YOU WANTED TO BE IN THE ENTERTAINMENT/ANIMATION INDUSTRY AND WHAT EVENTS LED YOU TO CHOOSE IT?

I always knew I wanted to be in entertainment, I just didn't really know exactly where. The animation industry was actually something I was really oblivious to. I didn't know anything about it. My internship at the Nick Animation Studio really made me love it though! I learned so much in those three months!

Q: WHAT DID YOU MAJOR IN COLLEGE? DO YOU THINK THIS HELPED WITH YOUR PURSUIT IN THE ENTERTAINMENT INDUSTRY?

I majored in Business Economics. Nowadays, I see that colleges have majors that are really specific and geared towards the entertainment industry. UCI didn't really have that, but my major was broad enough for me to pursue a lot of different things, including the entertainment industry.

Q: DID ANYONE/ANYTHING INSPIRE YOU TO FOLLOW YOUR PASSION FOR ENTERTAINMENT/ANIMATION?

I guess I just wanted to follow in my sister's footsteps, as she always worked in the entertainment industry (specifically music). It was Nickelodeon that opened my eyes about the animation industry and made me love it!

Q: AS AN EVENT MARKETING ASSISTANT, WHAT DO YOUR DAILY TASKS CONSIST OF?

In addition to helping out with all of the big tent pole events (Kid's Choice Awards, Kid's Choice Sports, Comic Con), the West Coast team handles all of the events happening for the studio. This includes catered meetings, employee screenings, speaker series, monthly art galleries, premiere parties for shows, holiday parties, department offsites, food truck visits, and so much more! I also am the official tour guide of the studio. This keeps us pretty busy.

Q: WAS EVENT MARKETING SOMETHING YOU ALWAYS WANTED TO PURSUE, OR DID YOU HAPPEN TO FALL INTO IT?

I actually fell into it. In college, I was never sure what I wanted to do. I worked at the events center in UCI and I liked it, so I thought I would try it out!

Q: WHAT'S THE DIFFERENCE BETWEEN EVENT MARKETING AND REGULAR MARKETING?

There is so much that goes into marketing, and so many departments that go under it. There's digital marketing, integrated marketing, sports marketing, and much more. Event marketing is just a subset of the overall marketing. It's just another way to promote the brand.

Q: HOW WOULD YOU DESCRIBE THE CULTURE AT NICKELODEON?

The culture is amazing, and it's why I love Nick so much! Everyone is so friendly, and we have plenty of events for our employees. We also have mentorship programs, speaker events, and Food Truck Fridays. You walk around the studio and everyone says hi or gives you a smile. It's a great and fun place to be at!

Q: WHAT HAS BEEN THE COOLEST MOMENT WORKING AT NICKELODEON?

It's really all been cool! It's hard to pick just one thing. All the events I've worked on are really cool. We hosted our first ever Nickapalooza [a celebration that Nickelodeon host for their employees featuring food, live music, and fun activities], and it was amazing to see all the employees come together to enjoy performances of fellow employees. We also made the studio courtyard look awesome!

Q: HOW DID YOU SCORE THE SPECIAL EVENTS INTERNSHIP AT NICKELODEON?

I just searched for special events internships on Google. I came upon the Nick Animation Studio website and applied. I went through two phone interviews and an on-site interview. To my surprise, I got the job!

Q: ANY ADVICE TO STUDENTS APPLYING TO NICKELODEON INTERNSHIP POSITIONS?

I would just say to apply everywhere, and don't be discouraged when someone says no. I've been told no plenty of times, but I always got back up and was determined to find an internship/job. Also, make sure to write relevant experience on your resume when applying for a certain job. My supervisor told me that one of the things they liked on my resume was that I had volunteered for the "Renal Prom" in high school, which showed that I had interest and experience in events.

Q: WHAT WAS THE BEST PART ABOUT BEING A NICKTERN?

I think one of the best parts was all the classes and events that were held for the Nickterns. Not knowing anything about animation, it really opened up my eyes. We had storyboard classes, resume writing classes, weekly screenings of the 90's shows that we grew up on, game nights, and lunches with show creators. It was awesome! We were able to network with other employees, and really bond with our fellow intern class.

Q: WHAT WAS THE INTERNSHIP EXPERIENCE LIKE OVERALL?

It was amazing! You are really treated with respect and as a fellow employee. All the classes and events were so helpful and inspiring. You're encouraged to network and have meetings with everyone, from VPs to PAs. If you're into animation, this really is a perfect internship!

Q: HOW DID YOU TRANSITION FROM BEING AN INTERN TO BECOMING A FULL-TIME EMPLOYEE AT NICKELODEON?

Timing was really on my side. When I was interning, the events team consisted of three full-time employees and one part-time employee. As I was graduating from UCI, one person from the team decided to move to another department. The VP of events decided to hire me as a full-time employee! It's really important to make sure you leave a good impression as an intern, because it could work out for you! I remember one of the employees told me that an internship is like a 3-month long interview, which is so true!

Q: WHAT WAS IT LIKE BEING A CREATIVE LICENSING/VIDEO PRODUCTION INTERN AT SONY MUSIC ENTERTAINMENT?

It was actually my very first internship and I think I was only a freshman in college, so I don't remember too much about it. I was very young and didn't know what to expect, so I didn't really take advantage of the opportunity. I didn't really network, which was my biggest regret. A lot of it was administrative work, like packaging and mailing content out. I also had to do a lot of research for music, which was cool!

Q: WHAT IS THE DIFFERENCE BETWEEN INTERNING IN THE MUSIC INDUSTRY COMPARED TO THE ANIMATION INDUSTRY?

I think my experience and age had a lot to do with what I thought about the industries. Being so young while interning for Sony, I wasn't determined to work too hard or get the most out of the internship. I thought it was a bit more intense and the atmosphere wasn't as friendly and inviting. But from what I hear, the internship at the Nick Animation Studio is like no other. Animation is super fun and the people are very friendly. I was really encouraged to meet with everyone to network, including executives. It was nice!

Q: WHERE DO YOU HOPE TO BE IN 5 YEARS?

I really do like working in events! In five years, I hope to just grow in the corporate event industry.

Q: WHAT IS YOUR DREAM PROJECT?

With Nick, I feel like I've been able to experience almost everything I wanted. I've been able to work on Kid's Choice Awards and Comic Con, which were events I dreamed of working on when I first started. It was also really amazing to work on the first ever Kid's Choice Sports. It's still my dream though to get slimed! There's also a lot of events that happen on the East Coast that I wish I could work on—like Worldwide Day of Play.

Q: WHAT HAS BEEN YOUR PROUDEST MOMENT SO FAR?

My proudest moment thus far has probably been the first event I officially planned and executed. I planned a party for the *Sanjay and Craig* crew last summer. It wasn't even that big of an event, but it was pretty special being my first one. Of course, something had to go wrong and the photo booth showed up a bit late, but other than that, everything went great!

Q: WHAT'S THE BEST ADVICE YOU CAN GIVE YOUR PAST SELF, KNOWING WHAT YOU KNOW NOW?

I'm pretty shy, so my advice to myself would just be to speak up more and to trust myself. Being so young, I felt like I should listen to other people's ideas as they had more experience than me. But I found out that companies are looking for new and fresh ideas from those who are younger!

Q: FAVORITE ANIMATED FILM AND/OR TV SHOW?

I love Miyazaki, and *Spirited Away* is one of my favorite animated films! As for TV shows, I've always been a huge fan of *Avatar: The Last Airbender*! I would actually get pretty star struck when I saw Mike and Bryan [creators of *Avatar: The Last Airbender* and *The Legend of Korra*] at work.

CPSIA information can be obtained
at www.ICGtesting.com
Printed in the USA
BVHW011939300619
552317BV00012B/195/P